Praise for *Quick and Easy Vegan Comfort Food*

"*Quick and Easy Vegan Comfort Food* is filled with accessible, invigorating recipes. Alongside simple preparation instructions are cooking tips and suggestions for pairings with other dishes in the book . . . Beautiful full-page color photos illustrate these delectable combinations . . . Simpson's unpretentious recipes provide vegan simplicity, and her enthusiasm for cooking is infectious . . . *Quick and Easy Vegan Comfort Food* delivers on all counts."

—**BRITTANY SHOOT**, Feminist Review blog

"With *Quick and Easy Vegan Comfort Food*, Alicia Simpson shows the budding vegan cook how simple it can be to whip up delicious, cruelty-free creations in the kitchen with common ingredients. The easy-to-follow recipes, creative meal ideas, and cook's tips are sure to inspire you to get cooking!"
—**LEIGH SALUZZI**, co-owner of Cosmo's Vegan Shoppe

"Alicia C. Simpson's book is a wonderful entrée into the world of vegan cooking for those who are just getting acquainted with what veganism has to offer, as well as those on a tight budget. *Quick and Easy Vegan Comfort Food* educates readers about yummy plant-based sources of protein, calcium, and iron—as well as how easy, cheap, flavorful, and quick it is to make healthy vegan snacks, smoothies, and dishes. This book is a must for those who have always thought 'going vegan' is intimidating, complicated, expensive, and time-consuming."

—**A. BREEZE HARPER**, editor of *Sistah Vegan*

"I love this book! As a vegetarian for over twenty-four years, I know the amazing benefits of a vegan diet for the person and the planet. I love how Alicia shares personal insights and delicious Southern-inspired recipes, making veganism easy and accessible to the masses. From the section on 'Vegan Myths' all the way to the decadent vegan desserts that remind me of mother's cooking, *Quick and Easy Vegan Comfort Food* has something for everyone. I highly recommend it to all of my readers!"

—**MARTHA THEUS**, 21st Century Vegetarians blog,
and coauthor of *"Throwin' Down" Vegetarian Style!*

THE EXPERIMENT

BECAUSE EVERY BOOK IS A TEST OF NEW IDEAS

Also by Alicia C. Simpson
Quick and Easy Vegan Celebrations

THE EXPERIMENT
NEW YORK

QUICK AND EASY

vegan comfort food

65 Everyday MEAL IDEAS
for BREAKFAST, LUNCH,
and DINNER *with Over*
150 GREAT-TASTING,
DOWN-HOME *Recipes*

alicia c. simpson

The Experiment, LLC
260 Fifth Avenue
New York, NY 10001-6408
www.theexperimentpublishing.com

Library of Congress Control Number: 2009927867
ISBN 978-1-61519-005-8
Ebook ISBN 978-1-61519-109-3

Cover design by Susi Oberhelman
Cover photograph by StockFood & Snowflake Studios
Author photograph by Cristina Harris
Photo-insert food styling and photography by Lori Maffei

Designed by Pauline Neuwirth, Neuwirth and Associates, Inc.

Manufactured in the United States of America
Distributed by Workman Publishing Company, Inc.
Distributed simultaneously in Canada by Thomas Allen & Son Ltd.

First published October 2009

10 9 8

Dedicated to my grandmother, Georgianne Little,
and my late nana, Inez Goodson.
Your strength inspires me. I love you.

contents

my long road to veganism

WHEN I WAS a kid my secret wish was to be a singer. But I couldn't carry a tune to save my life, so I moved on to more practical goals like being a pediatrician, a veterinarian, or a psychologist. Never in my wildest dreams could I have imagined that I would be sitting down to write my first cookbook, and a vegan cookbook at that.

If you look back on my childhood, I suppose all the tell-tale signs were there that that skinny, knock-kneed, energetic, animal-loving little girl would one day grow up to be a passionate vegan cook, but I never saw it coming. You see, I grew up in a house divided. As long as I've been alive my mother has never eaten pork and, sometime during my early childhood, I decided it would be a good idea for me to drop pork from my diet, too. However, my brother and father held fast to their bacon, ham, and pork chops. At the age of thirteen, when most kids are doing all they can to fit in and be cool, my girlfriend and I decided to stop eating beef. There was no rhyme or reason to it. She simply turned to me one day and said, "I think we should stop eating beef for the summer and see how it goes" and I said, "I think that will work." I never ate beef again. Seafood was not my thing, so at that point I was down to just chicken and dairy products. My friends and family all told me that I was on track to being a vegetarian but I swore that I would never give up chicken. I simply couldn't imagine life with no meat at all.

Flash forward to 2002, my senior year in college. I was observing Lent and I decided that this year I could think of no greater sacrifice than to give up chicken for forty days and forty nights. I went to the grocery store and armed myself with an arsenal of faux-chicken nuggets, patties, and anything else that even resembled chicken. From the first bite I was hooked. I turned to my roommate and exclaimed, "This is better than chicken! I'm never going back." At the end of Lent I found myself eating chicken once again. But something just didn't feel right about it, and by June I was officially a vegetarian.

By the age of twenty-one I had moved from my parents' home in California to college in Virginia, then to living on my own in Philadelphia. Now that I was a vegetarian people were constantly asking me how "strict" I was about my diet. I was frequently asked if I was a vegan or if I ever considered going vegan. My answer was always a quick and firm no. I was starting to become a bit of a cheese snob, dabbling in Gruyère, Brie, Asiago, and Jarlsberg. If it had an unpronounceable name and an unusual texture or taste, I had to try it. It just seemed like a ridiculous notion to give that up.

After only a year in Philadelphia I was uprooted to South Carolina, the land of pulled pork, spare ribs, and everything BBQ. The fact that I was a California-born vegetarian meant that I was just one step away from being a one-eyed, one-horned flying purple people eater to the good folks of South Carolina. When it was discovered that I was a vegetarian, the first questions were undoubtedly, "So does that mean you don't eat BBQ? No pulled pork? Nothing?!" I would shake my head in acknowledgment and they would clutch their pearls or gasp in horror. South Carolina wasn't exactly vegetarian friendly, and I quickly realized that my old habit of eating out almost every night of the week was not going to work anymore. I bought a bunch of vegetarian and vegan cookbooks and started experimenting. I liked many of the dishes I prepared from these books, but I wasn't able to find that many vegetarian recipes for the foods that I had grown up with and loved. I was born and raised in Fresno, California, which has some of the best Mexican food in the country. Although my mother's roots are in California, my father is from the Deep South of Alabama, so I grew up eating traditional Southern soul food as well. The very first recipe I came up with as a vegetarian was for tacos and my second was for collard greens. Two recipes led to three, and three to four, and before long, I had a spiral-bound notebook filled with recipes and splotched with food stains. I began to realize that I had the makings of a vegetarian cookbook.

After two and a half long years in South Carolina I made my way to Atlanta. By this time I had begun to warm up to the idea of veganism a bit more. Restaurants like Soul Vegetarian and Lov'n It Live showed me that vegan food could taste really good, but I still wasn't quite ready to take the plunge. Along the way, I found myself in a juice fasting class taught by Arden Zinn, the founder of a chain of popular juice and smoothie bars in Atlanta called Arden's Garden. One day she turned to me and said, "Why would you consume milk or its by-products? Cow's milk is made to grow a calf into a fifteen-hundred-pound cow or bull—not to feed an adult human." Suddenly it all just clicked for me. Out of all the compelling reasons to go vegan, for some reason that one statement did it for me. I quickly went home, tore out all the vegetarian recipes from my growing cookbook, and started working on the book that you are holding in your hands right now—*Quick and Easy Vegan Comfort Food*.

vegan myths

*t*HE TASTE OF cheese isn't the only thing that kept me from taking the leap from vegetarian to vegan. Countless myths swirl around veganism, and I think there's no better time than the present to just get them out of the way. I acknowledge that it might be a little odd to put vegan myths in a cookbook, but I promise I'll try to find a way to connect all of these to food.

The Famous Protein Myth

Well-meaning friends and relatives along with most anyone else in the omnivore world will inevitably ask you, "Where do you get your protein?" If you've only been a vegan or vegetarian for a short time, then this probably hasn't started to bother you yet. But give it time and it will. Here's some information to arm yourself with so that you can sound intelligent when answering that question.

A varied and well-balanced diet is the key to getting enough protein. Protein is in almost everything, except sugars and fat. If you maintain a diet with a wide variety of legumes, grains, nuts, seeds, vegetables, and fruits then you will likely get the protein you need. The chart on page 5 illustrates some of the most concentrated sources of protein. Some notoriously plentiful sources of protein are soy products as well as wheat gluten, also known as seitan. This list is far from complete, so do some research. You will probably discover that most of the foods you already eat are rich in protein.

FOOD SOURCE	PROTEIN (G)
½ cup vital wheat gluten flour	46
½ cup textured vegetable protein (TVP), dry	24
1 cup soybeans, cooked/boiled (edamame)	22.07
1 cup wheat flour, whole grain	16.41
½ cup sunflower seeds, without shell	16.4
½ cup almonds, whole	15.17
2 tablespoons brewer's yeast	14
1 cup wheat flour, white, all purpose, unbleached	12.91
1 cup cornmeal, yellow	9.91
1 cup peas, cooked	8.24
½ cup quinoa	8.14
1½ tablespoons Red Star nutritional yeast	8
½ cup pinto beans, cooked	7.7
½ cup kidney beans, cooked	7.7
1 cup spinach, cooked	7.62
½ cup black beans, cooked	7.6
½ cup navy beans, cooked	7.5
½ cup chickpeas/garbanzo beans, cooked	7.3
½ cup vegetarian baked beans, canned	6
1 cup broccoli, cooked	5.70
1 cup long-grain brown rice, cooked	5.03

Source: USDA Nutrient Database www.ars.usda.gov/nutrientdata, Bob's Red Mill www.bobsredmill.com/, and Red Star Yeast www.lesaffrehumancare.com/

Some of the values in this table can change based on the brand of product you are using, so check your labels.

Now that we've established that it's easy to get protein in a vegan diet, it's important to know how much protein you really need. The National Cattlemen's Association and the United Poultry Farmers have worked tirelessly to convince the American public that we need 60, 70, or even 80 or more grams of protein a day to live. However, for the average person, this couldn't be further from the truth. The World Health Organization (WHO) recommends .5g of protein per kg for the average adult (for your weight in kilograms, divide your weight in pounds by 2.2). The USDA RDA (Recommended Daily Allowance) recommends

.8g/kg for adults. Let's say you weigh 140 pounds. That means you need somewhere between 32 and 51 grams of protein a day. Looking at the chart on page 5, you can see how easy it is to get the protein you need.

Vegan Food Is Expensive

If someone tries to feed you this myth, then they are literally grasping at straws to make veganism seem as unapproachable and difficult as possible—which it is not. The fact is that vegetables are cheaper than meat. Even if you choose to eat organic foods, organic vegetables are still cheaper than organic meats.

Prepackaged, processed vegan food can raise your bill a bit, but as long as you don't make these items the staple of your diet you shouldn't break the bank. As an accountant's daughter, I've always kept careful track of how much money I spend on food a month. From my omnivore to my vegetarian days, and now to my glorious vegan existence, my grocery bill has barely budged, even with the addition of organic foods.

A great way to make cheap food even cheaper is to find local farms. From major metropolitan areas to small rural towns, local farms and farmers' markets are plentiful. Local Harvest online is a great resource to find local farms and farmers' markets in your area (www.localharvest.org/). Though I'm not a fan of the USDA, when it comes to supporting agriculture they do a really good job (www.ams.usda.gov/farmersmarkets/map.htm is a link to their farmers' market directory).

In this book you'll find the ⑤ symbol next to various meal ideas. This symbol is to note some of the more budget-friendly recipes in this book.

Vegans don't get enough calcium or iron

Getting calcium and iron in a vegan diet is actually very simple. The key to getting the right amount of any vitamin or mineral is to eat a varied diet. Change it up! Try not to eat the same thing more than two or three days in a row. The following are excellent sources of calcium and iron. I've also included links to websites that have pages and pages of calcium- and iron-rich plant foods.

6

FOOD SOURCE	CALCIUM (MG)	IRON(G)
½ cup sesame seeds	702	10.48
1 cup tofu, firm set in calcium sulfate	506	4.06
1 cup collard greens, cooked	357	1.9
2 tablespoons blackstrap molasses	352.59	7.17
1 cup orange juice with calcium	350	0.3
1 cup cow's milk, nonfat (for comparison)	302	1
1 cup soybeans, cooked (edamame)	261	4.5
1 cup spinach, cooked	245	6.43
¼ cup tahini	238	1.35
1 cup kale, cooked	179	1.22
½ cup almonds, whole	177	3.07
¼ cup raw almond butter	169	2.32
½ cup brazil nuts	112	1.7
1 cup swiss chard, cooked	102	3.96
½ cup sunflower seeds	83.5	4.87
¼ cup ground flaxseed	71.5	1.6
½ cup oats, instant	65.5	5.08
1 cup dried apricots	41	4.1
½ cup garbanzo beans/chickpeas, cooked	40	2.37
1 cup lentils, cooked	38	6.59
½ cup pumpkin seeds	29.5	10.33

Source: USDA Nutrient Database www.ars.usda.gov/nutrientdata

Some of the values in this table can change based on the brand of product you are using, so check your labels.

LINKS TO CALCIUM RESOURCES:

Physicians Committee for Responsible Medicine (PCRM) www.pcrm.org/health/veginfo/ vsk/calcium.html

Soy Stache www.soystache.com/calcium.htm

Calcium and iron are absorbed in the same area of our small intestine and therefore compete for absorption. If you choose to take an iron supplement, to maximize absorption, do not take them with any supplement containing high doses of calcium or with calcium-rich foods. Additionally, vitamin C helps increase the absorption of iron. A glass of orange juice with your iron supplement can help a little iron go a long way.

Above all, it is important to take care of yourself. A happy, healthy vegan is the best advertisement for how great it is to be vegan.

your new vegan pantry

WHEN PEOPLE ASK me what I eat, I usually tell them anything in the grocery store except the tiny little meat and dairy sections. Although that sounds pretty simple, there are a few ingredients that are staples of the vegan diet that, despite being somewhat common at traditional grocery stores, are easily overlooked by the casual shopper. Here is an introduction to your new vegan pantry.

Seitan

Seitan is made from wheat gluten, also referred to as vital wheat gluten. Gluten is the protein of wheat and is what gives wheat and other grains their binding properties. It is a favorite among vegans because, once prepared, it offers a meatlike chewy texture that pleases vegans and omnivores alike. Additionally, it is relatively inexpensive and very high in protein.

You can find prepared seitan in your grocer's freezer or refrigerated foods section—usually next to the tofu. Although store-bought seitan is convenient, I prefer the taste and texture of homemade seitan. The advantages of using homemade seitan are that you know exactly what's in it, you can shape it into anything you'd like (faux chicken breast, nugget shapes, or chicken strips), it's cheaper to buy a bag of vital wheat gluten than a package of store-bought seitan, and damn it, it just tastes better. The only downside to homemade seitan is that it takes about an hour to make. However, you can make a large batch and freeze it for later use.

Textured Vegetable Protein (TVP)

Textured vegetable protein (TVP) is made from defatted soy flour. Just ¼ cup of TVP contains 12 grams of protein and 15 percent of the recommended daily allowance of iron. At first glance TVP doesn't appear to be anything special. However, once rehydrated it takes on a texture similar to ground beef and can be seasoned to taste like anything you want. In this book I will always give you instructions on how to rehydrate your TVP and with what ingredients. But for a basic ground beef style, texture, and flavor, rehydrate 1 cup of TVP with 1 cup of dark vegetable stock and 1 tablespoon of hickory liquid smoke. This will make the equivalent of 1 pound of ground beef or turkey, perfect to add to Chunky Marinara Sauce (page 133), Sloppy Josephs (page 144), Mexican dishes, and Veggie "Meat" Loaf (page 173).

TVP is starting to show up more often in conventional grocery stores, and if your local grocer doesn't carry it, they can usually order it. TVP can almost always be found in most health and natural food stores either in the bulk section, the canned bean aisle, or the baked good aisle near the alternative flours. You can also find it online in various sizes and shapes.

Nutritional Yeast

Nutritional yeast is an inactive dry yeast, prized for its "cheesy" taste, and if you haven't already noticed, it's called for in nearly all vegan mac and cheese recipes. But it is more than just a cheese-tasting substitute; it adds a rich flavor and creamy texture to a range of foods, including popcorn, soups, casseroles, gravies, salads, and steamed veggies. It is loaded with vitamins, minerals, and 8 grams of protein for every 1½-tablespoon serving.

Nutritional yeast is available in the bulk section of most health food stores and co-ops and is fairly inexpensive. One important thing to make sure of when getting your nutritional yeast in bulk is that it is the Red Star brand. It has the highest vitamin and mineral content and, in my humble opinion, the best flavor.

Brewer's Yeast

There are two different types of brewer's yeast that go by the exact same name. One is the live yeast that is used in the brewing of beer and the other is a by-product of the brewing process that has been dried and killed, and is most often used as a supplement. Depending on the brand, some brewer's yeast can also be grown on beet molasses, which can up the nutrient value. Unlike nutritional yeast, brewer's yeast has a mild nutty flavor and is a great addition to shakes and smoothies.

Two tablespoons of brewer's yeast contains 14 grams of protein, 7 grams of fiber, and is a good source of copper, zinc, manganese, potassium, chromium, selenium, phosphorus, and the B-complex vitamins. You can find brewer's yeast near the supplements in most health food and traditional grocery stores.

Silken Tofu

You are probably at least vaguely familiar with tofu. Tofu has gotten a pretty bad rap by the American public but it is actually a very versatile soy product that comes in various textures that mimic the taste of whatever it is cooked with. Its texture lends itself perfectly to dishes like Tofu Scramble (page 67) and shows its versatility as tofu ricotta for Spinach Lasagna (page 154) and as faux fish in Filet o' Tofish Sandwiches (page 134). Typically tofu comes in soft, firm, extra firm, and super firm (although super firm tofu is typically found only on the West Coast of the United States). But all tofus are not the same. Silken tofu is a Japanese-style tofu that, as the name implies, has a softer, more delicate texture than traditional tofu. Silken tofu usually comes aseptically packaged and therefore is not typically found in the same part of the grocery store as refrigerated tofu. You can usually find it in the same aisle as Asian foods. Silken tofu comes in soft, firm, and extra firm and works well to create sauces like the Alfredo sauce in Fettuccine Alfredo Two Ways (page 130) and even to make Spinach Omelettes (page 70). It can also be used to make soy-based ice creams, creamy dips, as an egg replacer in baked recipes, and as a good substitute for soy yogurt.

Vegan Cheese

Although "vegan cheese" sounds like an oxymoron, over time I have come to love vegan cheese even more than I did its dairy-based counterparts. Vegan cheeses are beginning to show up more and more in conventional grocery stores and have been a fixture in health food stores for some time now. The key is to do a thorough ingredient list search for animal by-products such as casein and whey. Not all vegan cheeses melt, so look for a brand that is labeled "meltable" if using it in a recipe like Vegetable Lasagna (page 156) or Avocado Melt Panini (page 119). Here is a quick list of my preferred brands of vegan cheese:

- Cheezly – Mature White Cheddar, Meltable Mozarella, Garlic and Herb
- Sheese – Blue Cheese Syle
- Tofutti – Meltable Mozarella Slices
- Follow Your Heart – Meltable Monterey Jack and Cheddar
- Galaxy Foods Vegan Cheese – American Slices

If you can't find vegan cheese at your local grocery store, there are plenty of options available online at Cosmo's Vegan Shoppe (www.cosmosveganshoppe.com) or Vegan Essentials (www.veganessentials.com). You can also head to my blog Vegan Guinea Pig (http://veganguineapig.blogspot.com) for updates and reviews on vegan cheese.

Liquid Smoke

Liquid smoke adds the distinct taste of outdoor grilling to indoor cooking. In vegan foods it adds a "meaty" flavor without being overpowering. In this book it is most often used when flavoring textured vegetable protein, to give it that hickory outdoor smoky flavor and to dishes like collard greens where pork or smoked turkey are traditionally used to the flavor the greens. Liquid smoke comes in four flavors: hickory, mesquite, pecan, and apple. Most grocers typically only carry the hickory and mesquite flavors. You can find liquid smoke in most grocery stores in the condiment aisle near the steak sauce.

Vegan Worcestershire Sauce

Traditional Worcestershire sauce contains anchovies so it is a no-no for vegans and vegetarians. However, vegan Worcestershire sauce has begun to pop up in health food stores and some conventional grocery stores. You can usually find it near the liquid smoke in the condiments aisle. Depending on the brand, your sauce might say vegetarian or vegan but they are, indeed, both vegan.

Flaxseed

Flax was among the earliest domesticated plants. Flaxseed is a versatile seed that can now be found in many forms, including whole flaxseeds, ground flaxseed, golden flaxseed, and flaxseed oil. Flax is high in the essential fatty acid omega-3, protein, and fiber. Omega-3 fatty acids contribute to brain and heart health; they can't be made by the body and thus are an essential part of a vegan and omnivore diet. Whole flaxseeds are indigestible to humans, therefore ground flaxseed is preferable. To get the highest nutrient content from your flaxseeds buy them whole and use a coffee or spice grinder to grind the seeds as needed. Additionally, whole and ground flaxseeds should be stored in the refrigerator to increase their shelf life and keep their omega-3 content at its highest potency. Flaxseeds can be found in most traditional grocery stores and health food stores.

Flax Oil

Flax oil is oil that has been extracted from the flaxseed. If there is one thing that you should splurge on it is flax oil. It tends to be a little pricey, as high as $17 for a 16-ounce bottle, but for the health benefits alone it is worth the price.

Flax oil is easy to incorporate into salad dressings and dips, and to toss steamed vegetables with instead of using margarine. Like flaxseeds, flax oil is high in the essential fatty acid omega-3 and is often supplemented with additional omega-3s and lignans (a type of antioxidant). It is very important that you do not cook with flax oil or expose it to high temperatures, as this will destroy the oil's properties. Additionally, like flaxseeds, it should be stored in the refrigerator to maintain its integrity. Flax oil is typically found refrigerated near the probiotics in health food stores. It is starting to show up in conventional grocery stores as well.

Spirulina Powder

Spirulina is a type of blue-green algae that is often sold as a nutritional supplement in tablet, powder, or flake form. It is high in protein, vitamin A, B-complex vitamins, and iron. Although it also contains a large amount of vitamin B_{12} there is still much debate about the human body's ability to assimilate this B_{12} as readily as it can other B_{12} supplements. Spirulina is rich in gamma linolenic acid (GLA), an essential fatty acid that is important for brain, bone, and skin health, as well as in the regulation of metabolism. Spirulina can be found in most health food stores and traditional grocery stores in the supplement section.

Panko Bread Crumbs

Panko bread crumbs are a Japanese-style bread crumb, commonly found in the Asian food aisle of conventional grocery stores and health food stores. The main difference between panko bread crumbs and regular bread crumbs is the texture. Panko has a lighter, crisper texture that gives the perfect crunch to oven-fried foods like Oven-fried Chik'n Seitan (page 140) and the Filet o' Tofish Sandwich (page 134).

Blackstrap Molasses

It is a little-known fact that there are actually five different types of molasses. However, you typically see only two kinds sold commercially—cooking molasses (which is usually just referred to as molasses) and blackstrap molasses (also known as unsulphured blackstrap molasses). Blackstrap molasses is a by-product of the sugar-making process and has a slightly bitter, yet sweet flavor. It is rich in iron, vitamin A, and calcium. One tablespoon provides 20 percent of the recommended daily allowance of each of these nutrients. Blackstrap molasses is found in the same aisle as cooking molasses, near the sugar, in most grocery stores and health food stores.

Dairy-free Milk Substitutes

No discussion about nondairy milks is complete without a quick lesson on human nutrition. When humans are born, we drink our mother's human milk. It is perfectly designed to give us all the vitamins, minerals, protein, carbohydrates, and fat we need to grow from healthy infants into toddlers and beyond. Typically, we begin to transition to solid foods at around six months old—hence, we grow teeth. But for some reason humans revert to drinking milk and milk by-products, but it's not human milk we go back to, it's cow's milk.

Let's explore bovine nutrition for a second. When a calf is born it drinks the milk of its mother, a cow. This milk is perfectly designed to grow a calf into a 1500-pound cow or bull. As you might imagine, to get to that kind of weight you need a lot of protein, a whole lot of fat, and tons of carbohydrates (lactose). Cow's milk is so rich in all these nutrients that to give it to a human baby would have disastrous effects, such as iron deficiency and internal bleeding. Even though cow's milk has the right proportion of vitamins and minerals for a calf, it does not have the right proportion of vitamins needed for humans. It contains too few essential vitamins and minerals, such as vitamin E, zinc, and iron. And it contains too much sodium, potassium, and chloride, which can wreak havoc on a human baby's kidneys. To put it simply, cow's milk is made for calves and human's milk is made for humans.

A common milk myth is that cows make milk just for us to drink. This couldn't be further from the truth. Just like humans, cows begin to produce milk when they are pregnant and they continue to produce it until their calves are weaned. So why do all those dairy cows keep on producing milk? Humans inseminate the cows and keep them pregnant so they will continually have milk. But, as we have already established, cow's milk is for calves. What do these calves drink since humans are drinking their mother's milk? Unfortunately, the life of the calf of a dairy cow is pretty short and nutrition really isn't the main focus. Since humans are busy drinking the cow's milk there is just not enough left for the calf. Male calves are taken to live in a veal crates where they become "veal." They are put in a small crate with a little hole where their head can stick out. They can't move around, they can't run, they can't play or socialize. Instead they spend the remainder of their short lives eating a purposely nutrient-deficient diet to make sure the calf stays anemic so its flesh can be nice and white for the waiting human consumers. Why is this crate necessary? To prevent the calf from moving around. If the calf utilizes his muscles they will become stronger and therefore "tougher." Consumers want their veal flesh soft, so the calf is fed a diet so devoid of essential nutrients that it will attempt to consume its own feces and urine in order to get the vital nutrients it needs—which is why its head is tethered in place. Female calves are fed a mix of formula and milk so they can one day replace their mothers on the production line. It's time to put this myth to rest—cows don't just magically produce milk. They produce it for the same reasons humans do, to feed their babies. The only thing is, they never get the chance to nurse their male calves and most of these males never get a chance to grow up and become bulls.

The great news is there is a plethora of dairy-free, cruelty-free substitutes for cow's milk. In this book I use mainly soy milk and oat milk. Most recipes will work fine with either one. Recipes that work best with one specific type of milk are denoted.

Soy Milk

Soy milk is undoubtedly the most popular nondairy milk on the market. I can think of at least eight different brands off the top of my head, which come in a diverse array of flavors. You have original/plain, vanilla, very vanilla, chocolate, "egg" nog, peppermint, strawberry—the list goes on and on. My basic rule of soy milk is to use unsweetened plain for most of my recipes. The only exception to this is desserts, where I typically use the regular (full sugar) plain soymilk. But if stocking your refrigerator or pantry with two different types of soy milk doesn't sound appealing, I would recommend just using the plain/full sugar soy milk.

There are so many brands of soy milk out there that it's hard to know which one to buy. I stick to the rule of simplicity. The brand with the fewest number of ingredients wins. What more could soy milk need than soy beans, water, cane sugar, and maybe a little vanilla? Everything outside of that is just fancy

QUICK AND EASY VEGAN COMFORT FOOD

decoration. Keep it simple and organic or free from GMO (genetically modified) soybeans, and you can't go wrong.

Soy Creamer

Soy creamer is an excellent substitute for half-and-half, cream, and whole milk in recipes. It also comes in a variety of flavors, including plain, French vanilla, and hazelnut. But for the purposes of this book you'll only need the plain soy creamer.

Oat Milk

Trying oat milk for the first time is a life-changing experience, especially for a new vegan who is, typically, still heavily dependent on soy-based foods. Oat milk can be used anywhere you would typically use cow's milk or soy milk. It bakes well, tastes great on cereals, and cooks perfectly. It is aseptically packed for freshness, giving it a long shelf life. When I catch some on sale I stock up. There are usually no less than five boxes of oat milk in my pantry at any given time. It comes in plain/original and vanilla. Both taste delicious but I only recommend the plain/original for use in recipes. And as a side note, both also make an excellent hot chocolate.

Nut Milk

Nut milks such as almond and hazelnut have a sweet and creamy texture. Although they can be used for baking I typically don't recommend it. They are thinner and less nutrient dense than oat and soy milks. They are great chilled or with cereal and go well with coffee and tea, but that's where it ends with these nondairy milks.

Rice Milk

Rice milk is the second most popular nondairy milk. It bakes better than nut milks but not nearly as well as oat milk and soy milk. The taste is light and it goes perfectly with a big bowl of cereal and you can use it to make sauces. However, overall, I'm not a huge fan of rice milk. Although it is a good alternative to cow's milk it is not as nutrient dense as soy milk and oat milk. It has very little protein and a lot of sugar. If you're someone who likes to drink nondairy milk right out of the fridge, this is the milk for you. But as an all-purpose milk substitute, it falls short.

Hemp Milk

Hemp milk started showing up on the shelves of my co-op about a year ago. Its price tag turned me off for quite a while, but the aseptic box boasted its high omega-3 content as well as its complete protein profile. There are also claims that hemp protein is better assimilated in the body than soy protein. The taste is very nutty, almost like a mix of sunflower seeds, pumpkin seeds, and almonds. It's great on cereals and as a creamer for coffee and tea, but the taste is very strong and comes through in cooking. Some people don't mind the added nutty taste in their dishes and some people do. I'd say to try it in a recipe that is fairly inexpensive to see if you like the taste. Out of all the nondairy milk options, this is the most expensive, so experiment wisely.

Homemade Egg Replacers

There are some phenomenal powdered egg replacers currently on the market. Ener-G Egg Replacer is one of the most widely available and it can be found at most grocery stores and health food stores, along with other powdered egg replacers. I use powdered egg replacers, like Ener-G, in my recipe for Sweet Potato Waffles (page 52) and Peach Fritters (page 212).

Although powdered egg replacers are inexpensive and easy to use, if you don't have them on hand you can always use homemade egg replacers. Here's a quick guide to replacing eggs in any recipe.

As a substitute for one egg use one of the following:

- 2 tablespoons potato starch or corn starch
- 3 tablespoons to ¼ cup unsweetened applesauce
- 1 tablespoon ground flaxseed simmered in 3 tablespoons water
- 1 teaspoon baking powder plus 1 tablespoon white vinegar
- ¼ cup soft silken tofu, pureed in a blender or food processor
- ¼ cup plain soy yogurt

Butter-flavored Shortening

Many of the baked goods in this book call for butter-flavored shortening. Currently, the only butter-flavored shortening on the market in the United States is the Crisco brand. The ingredients list does not have any obvious dairy products in it; however, it does say that it includes "natural and artificial butter flavors." This led me to wonder if these "natural and artificial butter flavors" originated from animal products. I called The J.M. Smucker Company to see if I could find out. They promptly returned my call. The representative made it clear that there are no animal products in any of their shortenings. However, they did state that there is a small possibility that there may be traces of lactose in the natural butter flavor due to shared production equipment. The choice on whether or not to use butter-flavored shortening is a personal one. When I first began experimenting with vegan baking I used butter-flavored shortening in most of the recipes. However, I now prefer to use a margarine and shortening mixture of half nonhydrogenated margarine and half shortening. If it's a recipe that calls for something that is not easily cut in half, such as ¾ cup butter-flavored shortening, I usually use ½ cup nonhydrogenated margarine and ¼ cup shortening. Feel free to play around with the combination that gives you the taste and texture that is the most appealing to you.

The Grain Guide

Alternative Flours

CHICKPEA (GARBANZO BEAN) FLOUR

Chickpea flour is made from ground chickpeas (also known as garbanzo beans). Chickpea flour is a staple in Middle Eastern cooking and has increased in popularity in the United States because it is also a gluten-free flour. It has a high protein content, about 6 grams for every ¼ cup, and also is a good source of iron. Because of the recent boom in gluten-free products, chickpea flour is now showing up on the shelves of some conventional grocery stores, but it is still most often found in health food stores.

SOY FLOUR

Soy flour is a high-protein flour made of dried, ground soybeans. Like chickpea flour, it is also a good source of iron. Typically, soy flour can be found in the baking aisle or bulk bins of most health food stores.

SPELT FLOUR

Spelt is a sweet and nutty grain that is higher in protein, essential nutrients, and fiber than wheat. One cup of cooked spelt has over 10 grams of protein, 7.6 grams of fiber, 3.2 mg of iron, and 2.4 mg of zinc, according to the USDA National Nutrient Database. Spelt can be found in most health food stores. Make sure that you purchase whole-grain spelt flour. There are refined versions that do not have the same nutrient profile and also will produce a different texture in baked goods.

WHOLE WHEAT PASTRY FLOUR

Whole wheat pastry flour is a whole-grain, whole wheat flour that has been finely milled to mimic the texture of refined wheat flour. Using whole wheat pastry flour in place of refined wheat flour gives the foods you cook more protein, fiber, and nutrients, without sacrificing taste and texture. Do not substitute regular whole wheat flour for whole wheat pastry flour; the textures are very different and you will end up with a much denser product.

Cooking Grains

QUINOA

Quinoa (pronounced KEEN-wah) is not actually a grain but a "pseudo-grain." It has properties of both green leafy vegetables and cereal grains. Quinoa originated in South America where it was a prized grain among the Incas. The Incas were definitely onto something, because this little pseudo-grain packs a big nutritional punch. It is high in protein, and its protein is complete, meaning its composition of amino acids is ideal for assimilation in the human body. It is also high in fiber, iron, and other essential minerals. Quinoa is a versatile grain that can be eaten like oatmeal for breakfast or like brown rice as a side dish.

When cooking quinoa it is important to rinse it first in water. The outer layer of quinoa is covered in saponins, which gives the grain a bitter flavor. Although most commercial brands of quinoa are already prerinsed I always like to give it another quick rinse, just in case. To do so, pour the quinoa into a fine-mesh colander or strainer and rinse, shaking off any additional water. To cook, bring 2 cups of water or vegetable stock to a boil and stir in 1 cup of quinoa. Cook until the liquid is absorbed, approximately 15 minutes, fluff with a fork, and serve. This will yield about 2 cups of cooked quinoa.

BROWN RICE

Brown rice is a whole-grain, unbleached, unrefined rice that has a chewier texture than white rice. White rice is made by removing the husk, bran, and endosperm of the rice grain. This depletes several nutrients, such as B-complex vitamins, iron, and other important minerals, and fiber. Brown rice is produced by removing only the husk of the rice and therefore maintaining its nutrient profile. Because brown rice has two extra layers (the bran and the endosperm) it takes longer to cook than white rice. To cook brown rice, put 1 cup of rice and 2 cups of vegetable stock or water in a small pot. Bring to a boil, then reduce heat and simmer, covered, for 50 minutes, being careful not to remove the lid. Once the rice has finished cooking, fluff with a fork and serve. This will yield about 3 cups of brown rice.

JASMINE RICE

Jasmine rice is a long-grain, fragrant rice with its origins in Thailand. Its flavorful aroma makes it a wonderful alternative to traditional white rice. To cook jasmine rice, put 1 cup of jasmine rice and 1½ cups of water in a small pot and bring to a boil. Reduce heat, cover, and simmer for 20 minutes. Fluff with a fork and serve. This will yield 3 cups of jasmine rice.

JASMINE BROWN RICE

Like brown rice, jasmine brown rice is jasmine rice that still has its bran and endosperm intact while offering the same wonderful fragrance as white jasmine rice. Like other kinds of brown rice, jasmine brown rice also takes longer to cook. To prepare jasmine brown rice, put 1 cup of rice and 2 cups of water into a small pot and bring to a boil. Reduce heat and simmer, covered, for 45 minutes. Fluff with a fork and serve. This will yield 3 cups of jasmine brown rice.

Vegetable Stock vs. Vegetable Broth

I use vegetable stock in this book quite a bit. When you head to your local grocery store to look for vegetable stock, however, you might find only vegetable broth. Don't worry—the terms vegetable stock and vegetable broth are virtually interchangeable. What is important is the type of vegetable broth or stock you choose. All the recipes in this book, aside from rehydrated TVP, are made with light vegetable stocks, which are light-colored, thin stocks as opposed to darker, thicker stocks. The only exception to this is for TVP. When rehydrating TVP I prefer to use a darker, richer vegetable stock to bring out a bolder flavor.

Fresh vs. Dried Herbs, Seeds, Spices, and Seasoning

Using the right ingredients will make or break your dish. Here is a helpful guide to where and when to use fresh ingredients versus dried.

Garlic

I know it's tempting. A recipe calls for three cloves of minced garlic and you're just not in the mood to get out the cutting board, peel the garlic, and get garlic oil all over your hands. Well, tough! That jarred factory-minced garlic will completely change the flavor of your dish. Please, I beg you, don't even waste your money on the jarred or canned stuff. Please!

I would never tell you not to do something, then not give you an alternative. I recommend getting a mini food processor. You can make quick work of mincing just about anything with a mini food processor. You can even cheat and buy peeled, whole garlic to save yourself more time. There are also a lot of new garlic pressing, chopping, and peeling gadgets out there, so search around and you'll find everything you need.

Ginger

Ginger can be an intimidating root. It may seem hard to peel and chop, but with a paring knife or vegetable peeler you can have your ginger peeled and minced in no time. Although you can now find preminced ginger in jars and cans, resist the temptation and steer clear of the canned and jarred varieties. Nothing can compare to the taste and aroma of fresh ginger. As with garlic, to cut down on the chopping time of ginger use a mini food processor to mince fresh ginger.

Herbs, Seeds, Spices, and Seasoning

I know this sounds like the absolute opposite of everything you've ever heard, but when it comes to herbs, seeds, spices, and seasonings, fresh isn't always best. When cooked for long periods of time, fresh herbs tend to lose their flavor and are best when added at the very end of cooking. Dried herbs, seeds, spices, and seasonings are flavorful, store well, and, best of all, they are inexpensive. Although I am an advocate of fresh garlic over jarred garlic I do think that seasonings like garlic powder and onion powder add a concentrated kick of flavor to dishes like Vegan Ranch Dressing (page 184), Down-home Chili (page 129), Mac and Cheeze (page 84) and Spinach Omelette (page 80), to name just a few. Some common dried herbs, seeds, spices, and seasonings that are utilized frequently in this cookbook are:

Ground cumin
Turmeric
Garlic powder
Onion powder
Thyme (dried, not ground)
Sage (dried, not ground)
Oregano (dried, not ground)
Paprika

greatest inventions of all time!

tHE WHEEL, SLICED bread, and electricity pale in comparison to the culinary genius of kitchen gadgets. Here are some you just shouldn't live without.

Knives

Contrary to popular belief, you don't need an entire knife set to be a master chef or even a good cook. If there's one thing (actually two things) you're going to invest your money in for the kitchen it should be knives. The first two are must-haves; the last one is optional.

- 8-inch chef's knife or santoku knife: the most important item in your arsenal. This is going to be your all-purpose dicing, chopping, mincing, and slicing knife.
- 3-inch paring knife: this knife will quickly peel fruits or vegetables as well as slice like nobody's business.
- A serrated knife: In a perfect world you should have a 10-inch serrated bread knife and a 6-inch serrated edge knife to cut acidic foods like tomatoes and citrus foods (these foods will dull your chef's knife pretty quickly). Although these are both great things to have, you can get by with a cheap serrated steak knife. Since "steak knife" sounds really "unvegan" we'll call it the "seitan knife" for now. So you have two options: one cheap seitan knife or two expensive serrated knives. The cheap one won't last as long but it will get the job done.

- Knife sharpener – it's always a good idea to have a knife sharpener around. A dull knife is a dangerous knife. The dull edge of a chef's knife can easily slip and slide off the smooth surfaces of fruits and vegetables, and there's nothing worse than an airborne knife, so keep a sharpener on hand.

Baking and Casserole Dishes

I am guilty of having way too many casserole dishes, cookie sheets, Pyrex dishes, pie plates, etc. You name it, I have it. I might have two. Or in the case of casserole dishes, three or four.

Some things you really need more than one of, and when it comes to baking equipment the rule of twos definitely applies. Here are some of the essentials you will need:

- Two 2-quart glass or ceramic baking dishes; one of them should be an 8×8-inch pan
- One 3-quart glass or ceramic dish
- Two cupcake pans
- Two 9-inch-round cake pans
- Two baking or cookie sheets

Blender

Blenders are for more than just smoothies. I strongly recommend that you have a high-powered blender on hand. They are expensive, but they last a lifetime and can cut down your cooking time considerably.

High-powered blenders, such as the Vita-Mix, have up to a 2- or 3-horsepower motor that can pulverize even the toughest foods, such as avocado pits or macadamia nuts. These blenders even allow you to make warm soups and dips, as the friction caused by the high-powered motor warms the food as it blends it. A high-powered blender is essential to creating my Green Smoothies (page 31), as they have the ability to completely break down the fibers of the vegetables used in these smoothies. High-powered blenders also make quick and easy work of grinding nuts in dishes like Cashew Nut Cheeze Dip (page 192), Almond Milk (page 72), and Vegan Ranch Dressing (page 184).

If a high-powered blender is not in the budget right now, make sure you get the highest-quality blender that you can afford. An immersion blender is also helpful for pureeing soups, but it's not necessary.

Food Processor

A well-stocked kitchen should have at least one food processor. A medium-size processor of 4- to 5-cup capacity should take care of all your general chopping needs.

Another great gadget to add to the collection is a mini chopper or mini food processor. They usually have a 16- to 21-ounce capacity and make quick work of mincing and dicing just about any food item.

Pepper Mill

Nothing beats the taste of freshly ground pepper, which adds a bold and complex flavor to any dish. I like to use coarsely ground black pepper as a garnish for dishes like Caesar Salad with Sourdough Croutons (page 98), Grilled Vegetables (page 81), and Fettuccine Alfredo Two Ways (page 130) but you can adjust most pepper grinders from coarse to fine to fit your taste. Although I like to use freshly ground pepper as a garnish, I prefer to use preground pepper when measuring pepper for dishes. Having both on hand gives you a versatility of flavor that you will immediately be able to taste.

Mandoline

Although not essential to a kitchen, my life would be incomplete without this glorious gadget. It thinly slices everything from onions for French Onion Soup (page 100) to apples and pears for an elegant presentation. Depending on your style of mandoline, it can also julienne or crinkle-cut fruits and vegetables, and cut potatoes for my all-time-favorite, waffle fries. Essentially, it makes virtually any dish look like it was made with little effort by a master chef.

HANDY MEASUREMENT CONVERSIONS

All the recipes in this book can be easily halved, doubled, or even tripled based on the number of people you are serving. Here are some standard measurement conversions to take the guesswork out of converting measurements up or down.

1 gallon = 4 quarts = 8 pints = 16 cups

½ gallon = 2 quarts = 4 pints = 8 cups

¼ gallon = 1 quart = 2 pints = 4 cups

⅛ gallon = ½ quart = 1 pint = 2 cups

½ quart = 1 pint = 2 cups = 16 fluid ounces

¼ quart = ½ pint = 1 cup = 8 fluid ounces

1 cup = 8 fluid ounces = 16 tablespoons = 48 teaspoons

¾ cup = 6 fluid ounces = 12 tablespoons = 36 teaspoons

⅔ cup = 5⅓ fluid ounces = 10 tablespoons = 30 teaspoons

½ cup = 4 fluid ounces = 8 tablespoons = 24 teaspoons

⅓ cup = 2⅔ fluid ounces = 5 tablespoons = 15 teaspoons

¼ cup = 2 fluid ounces = 4 tablespoons = 12 teaspoons

⅛ cup = 1 fluid ounce = 2 tablespoons = 6 teaspoons

½ fluid ounce = 1 tablespoon = 3 teaspoons

energy-boosting green smoothies

COMFORT FOODS ARE usually those stick-to-your-ribs foods that remind you of home, family, and friends. It's the food you turn to after a long day at school, work, or with the kids, or when you just need to put a smile on your face. To put it plainly, it's the food that makes you happy. Vegan comfort food gives you the advantage of eating the foods you crave, while still eating a plant-based diet high in fiber, protein, and nutrients.

However, the hallmark of comfort food has never typically been green leafy vegetables, collard greens and kale being the exception. Green leafy vegetables are high in fiber, vitamins A, C, E, and K, B vitamins, magnesium, potassium, iron, and calcium. In order to make sure I was getting the best of both worlds—comfort food and green leafy vegetables—I started adding a little spinach to my smoothies, then sprouts, kale, and other greens. I soon discovered what a profound difference it made in my day. Whether I had the smoothies for breakfast, lunch, dinner, or a midday snack I felt revived, energetic, and ready to take on the world.

Green Smoothies offer a quick, easy, and surprisingly sweet way to get in an additional one to two servings of vegetables a day, as well as fruit. High-powered blenders help unlock the nutrients that are trapped deep within green leafy vegetables, giving you access to more vitamins, minerals, and nutrients than you would get just by eating them.

Here are two words of caution when it comes to Green Smoothies: start slowly. I have put these smoothies in an order that will help your body slowly get acclimated to all the new fiber and nutrients. As delicious as these smoothies are, don't be tempted to gulp them down quickly. If you do, you might be running to the bathroom rather quickly as well. The longer you drink these smoothies, the quicker you'll be able to drink them. But once again, start slowly. Additionally, the detoxifying powers of fresh green leafy vegetables will most likely lead to the release of excess mucus you have been accumulating. So if you notice you're a little more "mucousy" for the first couple of days or even a week, don't be alarmed. If you've ever had wheatgrass juice, it's like that, but dramatically milder.

Just as with any food, it's important not to eat the same thing every day in order to get a wide range of nutrients. A four- to seven-day rotation of different Green Smoothies is best. As time goes on and you get more and more acclimated to your Green Smoothies, start adding more greens. For example, instead of two leaves of kale in the Strawberry Pineapple Green Smoothie (page 38) add three, then four, or instead of using 1 cup of watercress in the Berry Watercress Smoothie (page 33) add 2 cups.

Lastly, the addition of dates and agave nectar strongly depends on the seasonality of the fruits being used. Fresh fruits that are in season tend to be sweeter, so try using a little less agave nectar or fewer dates and add more as needed.

Here is a short list of fruits and vegetables by seasons as a guide:

SUMMER	FALL	WINTER	SPRING
Blackberries	Apples	Grapefruit	Apricots
Blueberries	Belgian endive	Kale	Carrots
Broccoli	Ginger	Lemons	Collard greens
Cucumber	Grapes	Oranges	Mango
Nectarines	Pears	Tangerines	Mustard greens
Peaches	Pomegranate	Turnips	Pineapple
Plums	Swiss chard		Spinach
Raspberries			Baby lettuce mixes
Watermelon			Strawberries
			Watercress

Basic directions for all Green Smoothies:

In a high-powered blender, blend all the ingredients together until completely smooth.

spinach mango smoothie

MAKES ONE 16-OUNCE SMOOTHIE

Fresh ingredients are a must in this smoothie, so break out your juicer or head to your local juice bar and get some fresh pear juice.

- 2 handfuls baby spinach
- 1 cup frozen mango
- 1 cup fresh pear juice

berry watercress smoothie

MAKES ONE 16-OUNCE SMOOTHIE

The ripeness of your pineapple will dictate whether or not you need to add agave nectar. A perfectly ripe pineapple will smell sweet and have a bright green crown and a golden yellow body.

- 1 cup watercress
- ½ cup frozen blueberries
- ¼ cup frozen raspberries
- ½ cup fresh pineapple
- ½ cup water
- 1 tablespoon raw agave nectar, optional

Sunny Side up

MAKES ONE 16-OUNCE SMOOTHIE

Sunnies are sunflower seed sprouts, typically found in health food stores. They are much larger than traditional sprouts, just as sunflowers are much larger than the average flower. Sunnies have a similar nutrient profile to their seeds except that they are also a green leafy vegetable. Sunnies are high in protein, vitamins A, D, and E, B-complex vitamins, as well as important minerals like iron, calcium, copper, magnesium, phosphorus, potassium, and zinc.

1 cup sunflower sprouts

1 large fresh or frozen pear, chopped

1 cup fresh apple juice

Cucumber Cooler

MAKES ONE 16-OUNCE SMOOTHIE

A Cucumber Cooler is the ultimate in refreshing summer drinks. There is something about cucumber and melon that just make you want to sit outside and watch the summer day go by.

½ large cucumber, peeled and seeded

1 cup cubed cantaloupe

2 Medjool dates, pitted

1 kiwi, peeled

½ cup ice

fruit salad Smoothie

MAKES ONE 16-OUNCE SMOOTHIE

Romaine lettuce blends seamlessly into this fruit salad smoothie. With the addition of a ripe banana and frozen strawberries, you have a sinfully sweet smoothie that tastes good enough to be dessert.

- 2 to 3 large romaine leaves, torn
- 1 medium ripe banana
- 1 cup frozen strawberries
- ½ cup water
- 1 tablespoon agave nectar

greeny-blue smoothie
MAKES ONE 16-OUNCE SMOOTHIE

Despite the name, it comes out a purplish color. But greeny-blue-purplish smoothie was just too long a name.

- 5 green leaf lettuce leaves, torn
- ½ cup frozen blueberries
- 1 pear, chopped
- ¾ cup fresh apple juice

buckwheat peach smoothie
MAKES ONE 16-OUNCE SMOOTHIE

Buckwheat lettuce is a microgreen that looks almost like sprouts and can usually be found in the same section as the sprouts in your grocery produce section. They have a delicate flavor and go well on sandwiches, salads, and, of course, smoothies.

- 2 ounces buckwheat lettuce
- 1 cup frozen peaches
- 1 ripe medium banana
- ½ cup water

Swiss Smoothie

MAKES ONE 16-OUNCE SMOOTHIE

I'm embarrassed to say that the first time I had Swiss chard was when I was experimenting with Green Smoothies for this book. I was so used to mixing it in these sweet smoothies that I had no idea what to expect when I actually took the time to cook it. I discovered it is delicious either way. Green or rainbow Swiss chard can be used interchangeably in this smoothie.

 1 to 2 large Swiss chard leaves
 2 nectarines, washed, chopped, and pit removed (or frozen)
 ½ Fuji apple, seeded and chopped
 2 Medjool dates, seeded
 ½ cup water

tropical cress Smoothie

MAKES ONE 16-OUNCE SMOOTHIE

Cracking open a coconut can be hard work, but it is worth it to add fresh coconut water to this smoothie. With all the sweet fruits, you will completely forget that there are any vegetables in this smoothie at all. It is sure to become one of your favorites.

 1 cup watercress
 ½ cup coconut water
 1 cup papaya nectar or juice
 1 cup frozen mango
 1 ripe banana

dandelion smoothie

MAKES ONE 16-OUNCE SMOOTHIE

When I first saw dandelion greens in my grocery produce section, I didn't know what to make of them. They looked like the weeds I had just plucked out of my front yard earlier in the day. Although the prospect of finding edible greens in your yard is tempting, I suggest leaving this one to the pros and selecting high quality, farm grown, dandelion greens from your local grocer or farmers' market.

    1 cup dandelion leaves
    ½ cup frozen peaches
    ½ cup frozen strawberries
    2 to 3 Medjool dates
    1 cup fresh apple juice

everything's tur-ni-up roses

MAKES ONE 16-OUNCE SMOOTHIE

Turnip greens have a light flavor that blends perfectly into smoothies. This one comes out a beautiful pinkish-red rose color and has a sinfully sweet taste.

    2 to 4 turnip green leaves
    ½ cup frozen strawberries
    ½ cup frozen raspberries
    ½ ripe medium banana
    1 cup fresh pear juice

strawberry pineapple green Smoothie

MAKES ONE 16-OUNCE SMOOTHIE

This is my preferred early morning Green Smoothie. It is sweet, has a rich green color, and the addition of protein powder makes it a complete meal in a glass. As previously mentioned, if you are using fresh, ripe, in-season pineapple, there may be no need for the agave nectar at all.

1 to 2 kale leaves (any kind), torn into smaller pieces

1 cup frozen strawberries

1 cup cubed fresh pineapple

½ cup water

1½ teaspoons agave nectar, optional

1 tablespoon unflavored protein powder, optional

banan-o-rama

MAKES ONE 16-OUNCE SMOOTHIE

The sweet blend of kale, banana, tropical fruits, and apple juice are good for more than just smoothies. You can blend these ingredients and pour them into Popsicle molds to make this into a frozen treat.

1 to 2 kale leaves (any kind), torn into smaller pieces

1 frozen medium banana

1 cup frozen tropical fruit blend (pineapple, mango, papaya, or guava)

1 cup fresh apple juice

mango-cranrugula smoothie

MAKES ONE 16-OUNCE SMOOTHIE

Outside of cranberry sauce and dried sweetened cranberries, I could never think of any other way to eat cranberries without the tartness overpowering my taste buds. The apple juice and sweet mango in this smoothie help balance out the bitterness of the arugula and cranberries to make a harmonious green treat.

1 large handful baby arugula

1 cup frozen mango

1 cup fresh or frozen whole cranberries

1 cup fresh apple juice

1½ teaspoonsraw agave nectar

broccolini tini

MAKES TWO 8-OUNCE SMOOTHIES

Broccolini is a hybrid of broccoli and Chinese kale, offering the best of both worlds. This smoothie is incredibly detoxifying, which is why it's the only smoothie that is broken up into two 8-ounce smoothies instead of one 16-ounce smoothie. Broccolini has a special affinity for breaking up mucus. Drink this smoothie slowly until you get used to it; feel free to store it in the refrigerator, and sip it throughout the day.

1 cup broccolini florets

1 cup frozen tropical fruit mix (papaya, mango, pineapple)

1 kiwi, peeled and cut into thick slices

¾ cup fresh pear juice

2 to 3 Medjool dates, seeds removed

65 quick and easy meal ideas

Wake Up with a Smile

You've heard it all your life: breakfast is the most important meal of the day. I know lots of people who start their morning with a bagel and coffee, but to me, that classic combo doesn't really count. A well-balanced breakfast is more than just a bagel. A true balanced breakfast needs fruit, a protein source, and even vegetables. Putting together such a meal might sound like a daunting task, but creating a home-cooked nutritious and balanced breakfast is easier than you think. Whether you're on the go or have time for a sit-down breakfast, these meal ideas will be sure to satisfy. Just add a piece of seasonal fruit or fresh berries and you have all you need to start your day off right.

Happy Sunrise
Spinach and Cheeze Scramble (page 68)
Easy Breakfast Biscuits (page 60)
    or Spelt Biscuits (page 62)

Nutri-Boost Breakfast
Carrot and Raisin Muffins (page 59)
Protein Power Smoothie (page 57)

Gone Bananas! §
Banana Pancakes (page 54)
Tofu Scramble (page 67)

Running Late
    Breakfast Power Smoothie (page 56)
    Bursting Blueberry Muffins (page 58)

Fast-Food Nation
    "Egg" MacGuffin (page 64)
    Tahini Coffee (page 73)

Tico Time ⓢ
    Gallo Pinto (page 66)
    1 cup of fresh pineapple

French Twist
    French Toast (page 55)
    Breakfast Sausage (page 50)

Morning Glory
    Sweet Potato Waffles (page 52)
    Spinach Omelette (page 70)

Comfort Food To Go

Although breakfast is the most important meal of the day, lunch is the meal that helps you get through the last three hours of school, make it through one more meeting at work, or take a short break from the bustle of the day. All you need is an insulated lunch bag or box and a thermos to bring the best of homemade comfort food with you for your midday reprieve.

California Fresh Mex ⓢ
    Fresh Mex Burritos (page 137)
    Fresh Corn Salad (page 103)

Avocado Madness
    Tomato and Avocado Soup (page 113)
    Avocado Melt Panini (page 120)

The ABCs of Lunch
    Alphabet Soup (page 94)
    Ultimate Grilled Cheeze (page 122)

Dill or No Dill 💲
Avocado Sandwich with Dill Sauce (page 121)
Plain Ol' Hummus with Carrot Sticks (page 183)

Soba Siesta
Spicy Soba Noodles in Peanut Sauce (page 153)
Miso Soup (page 107)

Fat Chance
The Fat Chick (page 159)
Blue Corn Chips with Guacamole (page 195)

Japanese Takeout 💲
Teriyaki Rice Bowl (page 167)
Miso Soup (page 107)

The Mean Bean 💲
Red Beans with Quinoa (page 149)
Garlic Green Beans (page 86)

Wrap It Up
Garden Wrap (page 180)
Baby Carrots with Cashew Nut Cheeze Dip (page 192)

Is It Chili in Here? 💲
Down-home Chili (page 129)
Green Salad (page 97)
with Thousand Island Dressing (page 186)

A Fishy Situation
Tuno Tempeh Sandwich (page 168)
Carrot and Celery Sticks with Dill Sauce (page 188)

Tuno Me Is to Love Me
Tuno Melt (page 169)
Green Salad (page 97)
with Blue Cheeze Dressing (page 185)

Deli at Your Desk
Simple Croissant Sandwiches (page 163)
Potato Salad (page 110)

A Corny Lunch
Coconut Corn Chowder (page 102)
Fresh Corn Salad (page 103)

Around the Dinner Table

Who has time to make a five-course meal every night? Half the time, I struggle to make two courses! Here are a number of easy solutions packed with everything you need for a complete meal in two or three recipes.

Baja California Dinner ⑤
Fool-Your-Friends Tacos (page 136)
Spicy Corn (page 89)

Ciao, Bella!
Vegetable Risotto (page 176)
Caesar Salad with Sourdough Croutons (page 98)

Mama's Home Cooking
Veggie "Meat" Loaf (page 173)
Smashed Potatoes (page 88)
topped with Mushroom Gravy (page 197)
or Sage Gravy (page 200)
Garlic Green Beans (page 86)

Southern Nights
Fried Chik'n Seitan (page 139)
Collard Greens (page 80)
Classic Cornbread (page 90)

Tofu of the Sea
Something's Fishy Tacos (page 165)
Fresh Corn Salad (page 103)

Enchilada Fiesta
Vegetable Enchiladas (page 127)
or Chik'n Enchiladas (page 127)
Spicy Corn (page 89)

Italian Simplicity ⑤
Lemon and Caper Linguine (page 150)
Steamed Broccoli (PAGE 82)

Chinese Take-In
Veganized Orange Chik'n (page 174)
over Brown Rice
Steamed Broccoli (page 82)

Game Day
Spicy Buffalo Bites (page 143)
Carrot Sticks and Celery with Blue Cheeze Dressing
(page 185)
Easy Oven-baked Fries (page 83)

Backpacking Through Europe
Fettuccine Alfredo Two Ways (page 130)
topped with Steamed Broccoli (page 82)
French Onion Soup (page 100)

Alicia's Chik'n and Waffles
Oven-fried Chik'n Seitan (page 140)
Sweet Potato Waffles (page 52)
Collard Greens (page 80)

Give Me That Fish
Filet o' Tofish Sandwiches (page 134)
Easy Oven-baked Fries (page 83)
Green Salad (page 97)
with Vegan Ranch Dressing (page 184)

Italiano Classico
Vegetable Lasagna (page 156)
Green Salad (page 97)
with Balsamic Vinaigrette (page 187)

Nacho Ordinary Dinner
Ultimate Nachos (page 124)
Back-to-Basics Black Beans (page 77)

Say Queso!
Enchiladas sin Queso (page 128)
Six-Layer Dip (page 182) and Tortilla Chips

Honey, I'm Home!
Hearty Slow-cooked Vegetable Soup (page 106)
Green Salad (page 97)
with Blue Cheeze Dressing (page 185)

breakfast

breakfast sausage

MAKES 12 SAUSAGES

QUICK AND EASY
MEAL IDEA:
FRENCH TWIST
(PAGE 41)

There's just something about waking up on a Saturday morning to the smell of sausage cooking on the stove, French toast next to it on the griddle, and a bowl of fresh berries waiting for you. The key to mornings like this is to make as much food ahead of time as possible. These breakfast sausages get an even richer flavor when refrigerated overnight and will be ready for you to reheat and serve in the morning for that perfect breakfast that is guaranteed to make you smile.

DRY INGREDIENTS:

2 cups vital wheat gluten

½ cup nutritional yeast

½ cup soy flour

2 teaspoons onion powder

1 tablespoon whole fennel

1 teaspoon pepper

2 teaspoons paprika

⅛ teaspoon cayenne pepper

½ teaspoon dried oregano

½ teaspoon sea salt

¼ teaspoon ground allspice

2 teaspoons garlic powder

WET INGREDIENTS:

2 ¼ cups water

3 tablespoons vegan Worcestershire sauce

3 tablespoons olive oil

1 tablespoon Bragg Liquid Aminos

Combine all dry ingredients in a large bowl. In a separate bowl whisk wet ingredients together. Stir wet ingredients into dry ingredients until completely mixed and a dough forms.

Form ¼ to ⅓ cup of dough into a log, approximately 6 inches long. Continue until all the dough is used. Place each log separately into aluminum foil, making sure that it is tightly wrapped (if you don't wrap the logs tightly enough, they will burst out). Twist the ends of the foil to seal.

Place the sausages into a steamer over boiling water and steam for 30 minutes. Cool, remove the foil, and refrigerate, covered, until ready to eat. Sausuages will keep up to a week in the refrigerator.

When you are ready to serve the sausages, slice the links diagonally into ½-inch-thick medallions and pan-fry in canola oil until lightly browned on both sides.

Sweet potato waffles

MAKES 10 WAFFLES

QUICK AND EASY
MEAL IDEA:
MORNING GLORY
(PAGE 41) AND
ALICIA'S CHIK'N AND
WAFFLES (PAGE 46)

In the American South the terms "sweet potato" and "yam" are synonymous. We use the same root vegetable for Candied Yams (page 79) as we do for Sweet Potato Waffles, Sweet Potato Soup (page 112), and Sweet Potato Pie (page 206). Although we use the two terms interchangeably, in reality, yams and sweet potatoes are two distinctly different root vegetables with varying taste, texture, and size. If you shop at a conventional grocery store you will probably find yams in the produce department. These yams are actually garnet sweet potatoes. At some specialty markets, co-ops, and health food stores you may come across jewel, garnet, or Japanese sweet potatoes. Garnet sweet potatoes are the ones that you will use to make these scrumptious waffles, as well as the other recipes in this book that call for sweet potatoes or yams. Serve these waffles warm with maple syrup or peach preserves.

2 cups unbleached all-purpose flour

¼ cup firmly packed light brown sugar

2½ teaspoons baking powder

½ teaspoon sea salt

½ teaspoon grated nutmeg

1½ cups plain oat milk or soy milk

2 egg-equivalent powdered egg replacer, prepared according to package directions

¼ cup unsweetened applesauce

¼ cup canola oil

1 cup garnet sweet potato puree

Canola oil or vegetable oil spray for waffle iron

Combine flour, brown sugar, baking powder, salt, and nutmeg in a large bowl and set aside.

One ingredient at a time, whisk the oat milk, egg replacer mixture, applesauce, and canola oil into the sweet potato puree.

Stir the sweet potato mixture into the flour mixture and thoroughly combine. The batter will be thick.

Preheat the waffle iron and grease it just before you are ready to put in the batter. Pour in enough batter to fill the waffle iron, allowing for some spread after the lid is closed. Cook the waffles until lightly browned and they have stopped steaming (about 5 to 7 minutes).

Cook's Tip:

For lighter, fluffier waffles you can combine all ingredients, except egg replacement mixture, in a blender. Transfer this mixture into a bowl and fold in the egg replacer. Additionally, you can use canned or fresh sweet potato puree. To make it fresh, roast 1½ pounds of sweet potatoes for 50 minutes, scoop out the flesh, and put it directly into the blender.

banana pancakes

MAKES 1 DOZEN PANCAKES

QUICK AND EASY
MEAL IDEA:
GONE BANANAS!
(PAGE 40)

Believe it or not, there is a song out there called "Banana Pancakes," by Jack Johnson. From the first moment I heard it I couldn't stop laughing and smiling. One Saturday morning while humming this tune I looked over at a banana ripening on my kitchen counter and it all came together. Banana Pancakes are much more than just a happy song. Enjoy these pancakes lightly dusted with confectioners' sugar or serve them with a conservative amount of maple syrup. They will be sweet, so taste them before topping them.

¾ cup unbleached all-purpose flour

¾ cup whole wheat pastry flour

¼ teaspoon sea salt

2½ teaspoons baking powder

2 tablespoons granulated sugar

1 tablespoon brown sugar

1½ cups plain soy milk or oat milk

1 teaspoon vanilla extract

1 medium size ripe banana, mashed

Vegetable oil for the pan

Combine the flours, salt, baking powder, and sugars in a medium bowl. Create a well in the center of the dry ingredients and add the soy milk, vanilla, and banana.

Stir together just until combined. Some lumps are okay.

Oil a griddle and warm over medium heat until hot but not smoking. Ladle the batter onto the hot griddle and cook until bubbles form on top, about 3 minutes. Flip the pancakes and cook until golden brown, about 3 minutes.

Growing up, my French toast was a favorite of my little brother. Nearly every weekend he would wake up and immediately ask if I could make French toast for breakfast. Since it was my favorite, too, I was always more than happy to oblige. Once I converted from vegetarian to vegan, I thought that my precious French toast was lost forever and would be just a memory. But after tinkering around in the kitchen, I came up with a recipe that, in my opinion, is even better than the original! Serve these warm with Grade B maple syrup.

MAKES 6 SLICES

QUICK & EASY
MEAL IDEA:
FRENCH TWIST
(PAGE 41)

1 cup plain soy milk or oat milk

¼ cup chickpea flour

¼ teaspoon ground cinnamon

¼ teaspoon grated nutmeg

½ teaspoon vanilla extract

Canola oil for the pan

6 slices whole-grain spelt bread or whole wheat bread

In a shallow dish, whisk together the soy milk and chickpea flour. Once the chickpea flour is well incorporated, whisk in the cinnamon, nutmeg, and vanilla until thoroughly combined. There will be little lumps left in the batter. Don't worry about them too much, just make sure the bigger ones are dissolved.

Heat a large skillet over medium heat and add enough oil to cover the bottom of the pan. The canola oil will be very important throughout this process. You will learn by trial and error what is too much or too little. Remember that the bread will absorb some of the oil so add a little extra in preparation for that.

Dredge each slice of bread in the soy milk mixture and add to the hot oil. Cook the French toast until each side is golden brown, approximately 2 to 3 minutes per side.

breakfast power smoothie

MAKES ONE 16-OUNCE SMOOTHIE

QUICK AND EASY
MEAL IDEA:
RUNNING LATE
(PAGE 41)

If you hit the snooze button three times too many and find yourself running out the door with barely enough time to get your shoes on the correct feet, then this smoothie is for you. It takes no more than three minutes to make and contains a boost of nutrients to help get your morning back on track. Flaxseeds are an excellent source of fiber, lignans, and omega-3 fatty acids, the soy yogurt provides a protein boost, and spirulina is a rich source of protein, vitamins A, B_1, B_2, and B_{12}, as well as calcium, iron, gamma-linolenic acid, and chlorophyll. Any frozen fruit will work well with this smoothie, but my two favorite combinations are mangoes with bananas and strawberries, and pineapple with mixed berries.

   1 cup fruit juice

   ½ cup plain soy yogurt

   1 cup frozen fruit

   2 tablespoons ground flaxseed

   1 tablespoon spirulina powder

   1½ teaspoons raw agave nectar, optional

In a blender, puree all ingredients until smooth. To make blending easier, pour fruit juice and soy yogurt into the blender first.

COOK'S TIP:

Apple, pear, pineapple, or mango juice go best with this smoothie. Fresh juice is preferable, but if it is not available, try pressed juices or juices without high fructose corn syrup or any type of added sugars or artificial ingredients.

protein power smoothie

MAKES ONE 16-OUNCE SMOOTHIE

This is my all-time favorite post-workout smoothie! I run anywhere from 5 to 7 miles a day, and usually halfway through my last mile I start craving fries and onion rings. Luckily, this smoothie is the perfect rescue, and with the added protein, which helps repair those overworked muscles, you know you can't go wrong. But if you're still craving fries (page 83) and Onion Rings (page 87), then feel free to skip ahead a couple of pages—there are recipes for them, too!

QUICK AND EASY
MEAL IDEA:
NUTRI-BOOST BREAKFAST
(PAGE 40)

1 cup fresh pear or pineapple juice

1 cup mixed berries or a mix of pineapple, mango, and strawberries

1 tablespoon spirulina powder

1 scoop plain soy, brown rice, or hemp protein powder

In a blender, puree all ingredients until smooth. To make blending easier, put fruit into the blender first.

bursting blueberry muffins

MAKES 18 MUFFINS

QUICK AND EASY
MEAL IDEA:
RUNNING LATE
(PAGE 41)

Growing up, I loved those boxed mixes of blueberry muffins with the dehydrated blueberries and ingredients that a PhD in linguistics couldn't pronounce. This version is 100% vegan and 200% delicious—moist and sweet without all the mystery ingredients and with the bonus of whole-grain wheat! Whole wheat pastry flour is just like whole wheat flour but is milled to a finer texture to give these muffins that "melt in your mouth" effect.

½ teaspoon sea salt

1 cup whole wheat pastry flour

1 cup unbleached all-purpose flour

1 tablespoon baking powder

¾ cup sugar

½ cup nonhydrogenated margarine, softened

½ cup unsweetened applesauce

1 teaspoon vanilla extract

½ cup plain soy milk or oat milk

2 cups fresh blueberries

Preheat the oven to 350° F.

Combine the salt, flours, baking powder, and sugar in a medium bowl. Make a well in the middle of the dry ingredients and add the margarine, applesauce, and soymilk.

With an electric mixer, or an extremely strong arm, blend the mixture until smooth. Fold in the blueberries.

Line a muffin pan with unbleached cupcake liners and fill each three-quarters full with batter. Bake until golden, about 25 to 28 minutes.

carrot and raisin muffins

Muffins are like cupcakes that are actually good for you. With these Carrot and Raisin Muffins you can truly have your cake and eat it, too. Not only are they chock-full of omega-3-rich flaxseed, they also have tons of fiber, protein, and vitamin A. When you add in the beta-carotene power of carrots and the sweetness of raisins you can't go wrong with this recipe.

½ cup unbleached all-purpose flour

½ cup whole wheat pastry flour

½ cup ground flaxseed

½ teaspoon baking soda

½ teaspoon ground cinnamon

½ teaspoon grated nutmeg

⅓ cup sugar

1 cup plain soy milk or oat milk

¼ cup canola oil plus more for the muffin pan

1 teaspoon vanilla extract

2 cups grated carrot (about 2 medium-large carrots)

¾ cup raisins soaked in warm water for 10 minutes and drained, soaking optional

½ cup chopped pecans or walnuts, optional

Preheat the oven to 400° F. Line a muffin pan with baking cups or lightly grease with canola oil.

Mix the flours, flaxseed, baking soda, cinnamon, nutmeg, and sugar.

Create a small well in the center and add in the soy milk, oil, and vanilla. Mix until there are no more clumps of flour or flaxseed.

Fold in the carrots, then raisins and pecans, if using.

Fill the muffin tins or baking cups three-quarters full. Bake for 20 minutes or until a toothpick comes out clean.

MAKES 12 MUFFINS

QUICK AND EASY MEAL IDEA:

NUTRI-BOOST BREAKFAST (PAGE 40)

easy breakfast biscuits

QUICK AND EASY
MEAL IDEA:
HAPPY SUNRISE
(PAGE 40)

For me, there is something about biscuits that make an ordinary breakfast into a real meal. Whether it's Southern-style biscuits and gravy or just biscuits with jam and margarine, it all spells breakfast to me. These biscuits can be refrigerated for up to a week, so I like to make a batch on Sundays and eat two for breakfast each morning until they are gone. Instead of warming them up in a microwave, I like to cut them open, add a pat of margarine to each side, and lightly toast them in a toaster oven just until the margarine has melted.

2 cups unbleached all-purpose flour, sifted, plus more for working the
   dough

1 tablespoon plus 1 teaspoon baking powder

1 teaspoon sea salt

2 teaspoons sugar

5 tablespoons nonhydrogenated margarine or butter-flavored shortening
   plus 2 tablespoons margarine (for Southern-style baking method)

¾ cup plus 3 tablespoons soy milk or oat milk

Canola oil for the pan (California-style baking method)

Preheat the oven to 425° F.

Put the flour, baking powder, salt, and sugar into a food processor and pulse three times to combine. Add in the margarine and pulse until it begins to look like cornmeal.

Transfer the flour mixture to a medium bowl and create a well in the center of the flour. Pour the soy milk into the well. Stir in the soy milk until the mixture forms into a dough.

Transfer to a flour-dusted work surface and knead gently for 30 seconds.

With a flour-dusted rolling pin, roll out the dough to about 1-inch thick. Using the biscuit cutter of your choice, cut out biscuits. Take the remaining dough, form it into a ball (do not knead it), roll out, and repeat until all the dough is used.

Southern-style baking method: Melt 2 tablespoons of margarine in a 9-inch round cake pan or baking sheet, in the oven. Coat all sides of the biscuits with margarine as you place them in the pan. Don't worry if the biscuits touch—that's really the idea. Bake for 10 to 12 minutes, until golden brown on top or a toothpick comes out clean.

California-style baking method: Place the biscuits on a lightly oiled cookie sheet, or a cookie sheet covered with parchment paper, about ½ inch apart. Bake for 10 to 12 minutes, until golden brown on top or a toothpick comes out clean.

Spelt biscuits

MAKES 1 DOZEN BISCUITS

QUICK AND EASY
MEAL IDEA:
HAPPY SUNRISE
(PAGE 40)

My curious nature leads me to wander up and down the aisles of my grocery store and co-op until I find something I've never cooked with before. It can be an expensive habit but a deliciously exciting one. I discovered spelt on one of my wanderings. Once I opened the bag of this dark-brown nutty flour, I knew that I had to make biscuits. What a great choice! These biscuits are light, fluffy, and sweet with a rich taste that will have you coming back for more.

2⅓ cup whole spelt flour

2½ teaspoons baking powder

½ teaspoon sea salt

2 tablespoons sugar

⅓ cup nonhydrogenated margarine plus 2 tablespoons margarine (for the Southern-style baking method)

¾ cup soy milk or oat milk

Canola oil for the pan (California-style baking method)

Preheat the oven to 350° F.

Put the flour, baking powder, salt, and sugar into a food processor and pulse three times to combine. Add the margarine and pulse until it resembles a crumbly mixture.

Transfer the flour mixture to a medium bowl and create a well in the center of the flour. Pour soy milk into the well. Stir in the soy milk until a dough forms.

Transfer the dough to a flour-dusted work surface, being careful not to knead dough to prevent biscuits from becoming too dense. With a flour-dusted rolling pin, roll out the dough to about 1 inch thick. Using the biscuit cutter of your choice, cut out biscuits. Take the remaining dough, form it into a ball (do not knead it), roll out, and repeat until all the dough is used.

Southern-style baking method: Melt 2 tablespoons of margarine in a 9-inch round cake pan or baking sheet, in the oven.

Coat all sides of the biscuits with margarine as you place them in the pan. Don't worry if the biscuits touch—that's really the idea. Bake for 10 to 12 minutes, until golden brown on top or a toothpick comes out clean.

California-style baking method: Place the biscuits on a lightly oiled cookie sheet, or a cookie sheet covered with parchment paper, about ½ inch apart. Bake for 10 to 12 minutes, until golden brown on top or a toothpick comes out clean.

"egg" macguffin

MAKES 2 SANDWICHES

QUICK AND EASY
MEAL IDEA:
FAST-FOOD NATION
(PAGE 41)

Transitioning from vegetarian to vegan was life changing in more ways than one. I'm the kind of girl who gets up at 8 a.m. when I have a 9 a.m. appointment across town. I love to sleep and will stay in bed as long as humanly possible. As a vegetarian this was no big deal because I could always stop at a fast-food restaurant, get a breakfast sandwich, orange juice, and hash browns, and be on my way. This probably wasn't the healthiest option for me, but it sure was the quickest. These "Egg" MacGuffins solve my entire morning problem. Now while I'm showering, dressing, and putting on makeup at lightning speed, these sandwiches are reheating in the toaster oven, so all I have to do is grab them and run out the door.

¼ cup plus 2 tablespoons firm or extra-firm silken tofu

1 teaspoon nutritional yeast

1 tablespoon unbleached all-purpose flour

Pinch of sea salt

Pinch of turmeric

Oil for the pan

2 English muffins

2 slices vegan American cheese

2 vegan sausage patties, cooked, optional

With a mini food processor or immersion blender, mix the tofu, nutritional yeast, flour, salt, and turmeric.

Heat a well-oiled skillet over medium heat and pour the tofu mixture into a small pancake shape. Cook about 5 minutes on each side, until just golden brown.

Lightly toast the English muffins and layer them with "egg," tofu and sausage.

The "egg" portion of this "Egg" MacGuffin can be made the night before, refrigerated, and reheated in a toaster oven. If you find that you fancy a MacGuffin more than once a week you can double, triple, or even quadruple this recipe and just reheat the "egg" every morning before you assemble your breakfast sandwich. The "egg" will last up to five days in the refrigerator.

gallo pinto

**MAKES 4 LARGE OR
6 SMALL SERVINGS**

QUICK & EASY
MEAL IDEA:
TICO TIME (PAGE 41)

Gallo Pinto is a traditional Costa Rican comfort food. This rice and beans dish can be served at any meal but is traditionally served for breakfast along with other staples such as scrambled eggs, or, in this case Tofu Scramble (page 67) with a side of fresh Costa Rican pineapple. You can also enjoy this dish for lunch or dinner topped with a little Pico de Gallo (page 199) and served with a side of Spicy Corn (page 89).

Two 15-ounce cans black beans, drained and rinsed

1 cup vegetable stock

½ cup diced Spanish or yellow onion

2 tablespoons diced bell pepper

1 tablespoons canola oil

1 tablespoon mesquite liquid smoke

1½ teaspoons vegan Worcestershire sauce

1½ teaspoons hot sauce

3 cups cooked white or brown jasmine rice

1 tablespoon cilantro, finely chopped

Warm the black beans and vegetable stock in a medium saucepan over medium heat.

Meanwhile, in large saucepan over medium-high heat sauté the onion and bell pepper in canola oil for 3 minutes.

Add the beans (including stock) and cook for an additional 2 minutes. Add the liquid smoke, Worcestershire sauce, and hot sauce.

Add the rice and cilantro, stirring well to combine. Cook for an additional 3 minutes, stirring constantly to ensure that the rice does not stick to the bottom of the pan.

Tofu Scramble is the scrambled egg of the vegan world. If you're skeptical about the taste and texture of tofu, this recipe is definitely a good place to start. If you are a fan of tofu, like me, this will truly be love at first bite!

You can serve this Tofu Scramble as is or add a Mexican twist by wrapping it into a breakfast burrito with salsa and cilantro.

MAKES 4 SERVINGS

QUICK AND EASY
MEAL IDEA:
GONE BANANAS!
(PAGE 40)

1 tablespoon canola oil

½ cup diced Spanish, white, or yellow onion

3 garlic cloves, minced

¼ cup finely chopped red or green bell pepper

1 pound firm or extra-firm tofu, drained and lightly pressed

½ teaspoon red pepper flakes

2 teaspoons ground cumin

1 teaspoon dried thyme

1 teaspoon paprika

½ teaspoon turmeric

½ teaspoon sea salt

½ medium tomato, chopped

¼ cup nutritional yeast

Heat oil over medium-high heat, add the onions, and sauté for 2 minutes. Add the garlic and bell peppers and sauté for an additional minute.

Crumble the tofu into the skillet. The chunks should be small to medium so they will cook evenly. Mix in the red pepper flakes, cumin, thyme, paprika, turmeric, and salt until tofu is completely coated.

Add the tomatoes and cook for 5 to 10 minutes, depending on the desired texture.

Remove from the heat, add nutritional yeast, and thoroughly combine. Serve warm.

Spinach and Cheeze Scramble

MAKES 4 SERVINGS

QUICK AND EASY
MEAL IDEA:
HAPPY SUNRISE
(PAGE 40)

Even as a vegan I find it challenging to eat as many green leafy vegetables as I know I should. I've started to eat my breakfast, lunch, and dinner with a side of something green and incorporate a Green Smoothie (page 31) somewhere throughout the day. This Spinach and Cheeze Scramble is a quick and easy way to start your day off with nutrient-packed greens. Two cups of spinach wilts down considerably, so if you want a bigger boost of greens feel free to add another cup or two.

1 tablespoon canola oil

1 medium shallot, diced

2 garlic cloves, minced

¼ cup diced cremini mushrooms, stems removed

1 pound firm or extra-firm tofu, drained and lightly pressed

½ teaspoon turmeric

1 teaspoon paprika

1 teaspoon dried thyme

1 teaspoon ground cumin

½ teaspoon Italian seasoning

½ teaspoon red pepper flakes

½ teaspoon sea salt

2 to 3 handfuls baby spinach (about 2 cups)

⅓ cup nutritional yeast

Heat the oil over medium heat, add the shallots, and sauté for 1 minute. Add the garlic and mushrooms and sauté for an additional minute.

Crumble the tofu into the skillet. The chunks should be small to medium so they will cook evenly. Add the turmeric, paprika, thyme, cumin, Italian seasoning, red pepper flakes, and salt until the tofu is completely coated.

Cook for 5 to 10 minutes depending on your desired texture.

Add baby spinach and cook until spinach leaves have wilted, about 2 to 3 minutes. Turn off the heat, add the nutritional yeast, and thoroughly combine. Serve warm.

COOK'S TIP:

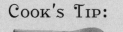

When you drain and press your tofu leave a little more water in it than you usually would. The additional water will help the tofu absorb the flavor of the herbs, spices, and seasonings.

spinach omelette

**MAKES 2 LARGE
OR 4 SMALL OMELETTES**

QUICK AND EASY
MEAL IDEA:
MORNING GLORY
(PAGE 41)

What is it about omelettes? When I was in college, students would line up around the cafeteria just to get a custom-made omelette. Even now, when I stay in a hotel with a good breakfast buffet, I can always count on coming downstairs to find people waiting patiently, stomachs growling loudly, to get an omelette. There's just something about an omelette that makes you feel at home, and that is the true essence of comfort food.

SPINACH FILLING:

1 tablespoon canola oil

¼ cup diced white onion

¼ cup diced red bell pepper

2 cups fresh baby spinach

OMELETTE:

12.3 ounces extra-firm silken tofu

1 tablespoon tahini

¼ teaspoon onion powder

⅛ teaspoon garlic powder

¼ teaspoon turmeric

⅛ teaspoon curry powder

1 teaspoon sea salt

2 tablespoons potato starch

1½ tablespoons nutritional yeast

2 tablespoons soy milk or rice milk

3 tablespoons canola oil

To make the filling:
Warm the canola oil in a medium saucepan over medium heat. Add the onion and bell pepper and sauté for 2 minutes. Add the spinach and stir constantly until spinach cooks down, about 3 minutes. Remove the pan from the heat and set aside.

To make the omelette:

In a blender, combine all omelette ingredients (except canola oil) until smooth.

Warm the canola oil in a large skillet over medium heat.

If you are making small omelettes, pour two small dollops of omelette batter into the oil and smooth it out with the back of a spoon, going from the center to the edge of the omelette batter until you have two uniformly round omelettes. If making large omelettes, pour one-half of the omelette batter into the oil and smooth it out as above.

Cover and cook for 5 minutes.

Add the filling ingredients to one half of the omelette and, with a spatula, fold over to create a traditional crescent omelette shape. With a spatula (or two) move the omelette onto a serving plate. If the edges of your skillet are shallow, you can try sliding your omelette out of the pan and onto your serving plate. Repeat until all ingredients are used up.

COOK'S TIP:

The smaller you make these omelettes the more uniform in shape they will come out. If you happen to break the form of your omelettes while folding over the edges, just add some vegan cheese or fresh salsa on top to hide the imperfections.

almond milk

MAKES 5 CUPS

QUICK AND EASY
MEAL IDEA:
TAHINI COFFEE IN
FAST-FOOD NATION
(PAGE 41)
SEE ALSO PAGE 73.

You can make this recipe using a variety of nuts. Almonds, cashews, and hazelnuts are my favorites, but experiment until you find one that is the right flavor for you. If you plan to bake with Almond Milk, make it with ¼ cup raw cashews and ¾ cup raw almonds, instead of all almonds.

1 cup soaked raw almonds

3½ cups filtered water

Pinch of sea salt

2 tablespoons raw agave nectar

1 teaspoon vanilla extract, optional

Combine all ingredients in a blender and blend on the highest speed until smooth. If you like, you can strain the milk through a cheesecloth, or just drink it as is. This keeps for about two days in the refrigerator in an airtight container.

tahini coffee

I don't like coffee but I love Tahini Coffee (and not just because I created the recipe). It can be served at any temperature you like for a year-round treat that is good for you. Tahini is made of hulled sesame seeds and is a great source of calcium and protein. Blackstrap molasses is a nutrient-dense sweetener that is especially high in iron and calcium. With the combination of tahini, blackstrap molasses, and soy, oat, or nut milk you get a powerhouse of calcium, protein, and iron.

1 cup plain soy milk, oat milk, or almond milk (page 72)

1 tablespoon raw tahini

1 tablespoon unsulphured blackstrap molasses

Dash of freshly grated nutmeg, optional

In a small bowl or coffee mug, whisk all ingredients together until thoroughly combined, making sure none of the delicious but sticky ingredients are left at the bottom.

For a warm version, whisk all ingredients together in a small saucepan over medium heat and bring to a very low boil. When it's hot enough for you, pour it into your favorite mug, sprinkle with a little nutmeg, and enjoy!

For an iced version, it's pretty self-explanatory—pour over ice and enjoy!

My favorite way to have this is at room temperature with the chill of the soy milk, oat milk, or almond milk being just enough. Try all three ways and find the one you like.

MAKES ONE 8-OUNCE SERVING

QUICK AND EASY
MEAL IDEA:
FAST-FOOD NATION
(PAGE 41)

the green goblin

QUICK AND EASY
MEAL IDEA:
NUTRI-BOOST BREAKFAST
(PAGE 40)
OR RUNNING LATE
(PAGE 41)
INSTEAD OF SMOOTHIES

As delicious as smoothies are, sometimes you just don't have time to find all the ingredients you need, take out the blender, and clean up when you're rushing out the door in the morning. The Green Goblin isn't pretty, but it hits the spot. I recommend making a big batch in the beginning of the week, or even the month, and storing it in an airtight container in the refrigerator so you can add a scoop of it to the juice of your choice anytime you like.

1 tablespoon ground flaxseed

1 tablespoon wheat germ, brewer's yeast, or almond meal

1 tablespoon unflavored protein powder

1½ teaspoons spirulina powder

1½ teaspoons psyllium seed

Fresh fruit juice

Add all ingredients to a 16-ounce glass, fill the rest of the glass with fresh fruit juice, stir (or shake if you have a lid), and drink quickly.

TWO WEEKS' WORTH OF THE GREEN GOBLIN

Just in case you don't feel like doing the multiplication, here's the 2-week version.

1 cup ground flaxseed

1 cup wheat germ, brewer's yeast, or almond meal

1 cup unflavored protein powder

½ cup spirulina

½ cup psyllium seed

Add all ingredients to an airtight container and refrigerate until ready to use. Scoop out one-fourth cup at a time and follow directions above.

side dishes

agave-glazed carrots

MAKES 4 SERVINGS

QUICK AND EASY
MEAL IDEA:
SLOPPY JALOPY
(PAGE 43)

Glazed carrots are a lighter alternative to candied yams that are also quick and easy to make. The carrots have a natural sweetness that is heightened by the orange juice and agave nectar.

6 medium carrots, peeled and cut lengthwise
    into quarters then into 1-inch pieces
¼ cup agave nectar
⅛ teaspoon ground cinnamon
1 teaspoon canola oil
¼ cup orange juice

Preheat the oven to 350° F.

Combine all ingredients in a 2-quart casserole dish.

Cover and bake for 15 minutes. Uncover and bake for an additional 15 minutes. Serve warm.

back-to-basics black beans

This recipe works well with all sorts of beans, not just black beans. Try it with kidney, pinto, black-eyed peas, or adzuki beans. They go nicely over brown rice, quinoa, or even pearl barley, to make a quick and easy meal.

6 garlic cloves, minced

1 tablespoon plus 1 teaspoon canola oil

Two 15-ounce cans black beans, drained and rinsed

1 teaspoon sea salt

1 teaspoon pepper

½ cup water

1 tablespoon plus 1 teaspoon canola oil

Sauté the garlic in canola oil in a medium saucepan over medium heat until it becomes fragrant, about 1 minute.

Add water, the beans, salt, pepper, and bring to a boil.

Lower the heat, cover, and simmer for 15 minutes, stirring occasionally. Serve warm.

MAKES 4 SERVINGS

QUICK AND EASY
MEAL IDEAS:
NACHO ORDINARY
DINNER (PAGE 48) AND
THE MIGHTY MUSHROOM
(PAGE 43)

maple-smoked baked beans

MAKES 12-14 SERVINGS

QUICK AND EASY
MEAL IDEA:
BACKYARD BBQ
(PAGE 45)

These beans aren't actually baked, but I guarantee they are delicious. They offer a sweet and smoky flavor without the use of the traditional pork or turkey. This recipe is large enough to feed an army or a backyard BBQ. But if you're serving a more intimate audience, you'll be happy to know it freezes well. If you have a smaller slow-cooker, feel free to cut the recipe in half.

2 pounds dried navy beans, picked over for stones,
   soaked overnight, and drained
2 tablespoons hickory liquid smoke
½ cup roughly chopped red onion
1 cup vegetable stock
3½ cups water
1¼ cups maple syrup
½ cup ketchup
1¼ cups packed light brown sugar
½ teaspoon pepper
½ teaspoon paprika
½ teaspoon garlic powder

Transfer the drained beans into a 5½- to 6-quart slow-cooker and add all the ingredients. Cook on low for 10 hours.

candied yams

Candied Yams are the quintessential side dish of every major holiday and a soul food staple of the American South. Sweet potatoes, as the name implies, are already sweet on their own. But add brown sugar or Sucanat (nonrefined cane sugar) and just the right amount of cinnamon and nutmeg, and the humble sweet potato becomes a classic Southern side dish that is always a crowd pleaser.

MAKES 4 TO 6 SERVINGS

QUICK AND EASY
MEAL IDEA:
SOUTHERN FRIED SPECIAL
(PAGE 45)

2 medium-large yams or garnet sweet potatoes, peeled and roughly chopped (approximately 1½ pounds)

¼ cup canola oil

1½ teaspoons vanilla extract

1½ teaspoons freshly grated nutmeg

¼ teaspoon ground cinnamon

¼ cup plus 2 tablespoons Sucanat or ½ cup packed light brown sugar

Preheat the oven to 350° F.

Place all ingredients in a large bowl and mix until the potatoes are completely coated.

Transfer the potatoes to a 2-quart baking dish, cover with aluminum foil, and bake for 45 minutes or until the potatoes are tender.

collard greens

MAKES 4 TO 6 SERVINGS

QUICK AND EASY
MEAL IDEAS:
SOUTHERN NIGHTS
(PAGE 44),
ALICIA'S CHIK'N AND
WAFFLES (PAGE 46), AND
SOUTH BY SOUTHWEST
(PAGE 47)

COOK'S TIP:

If you are in a hurry
and want your greens
now, forgo the last step
and serve immediately.

In the American South, collard greens are usually slow-cooked with pork or smoked turkey. After experimenting with a lot of different flavors to get that authentic Southern smoky taste, I discovered that garlic is the one thing that adds that authentic flavor.

1 pound collard greens (about 1 large bunch), washed

½ pound mustard greens, turnip greens, or kale, washed

1 tablespoon canola oil

5 garlic cloves, minced

5 cups vegetable stock

1½ teaspoons red chili flakes, or more to taste

1 tablespoon hickory liquid smoke

Roll several collard green leaves like a cigar and chop them into ½-inch strips until entire bunch is chopped. Repeat this with the mustard greens and set aside.

In a large stockpot, warm the canola oil over medium heat, add the garlic, and sauté until the garlic is fragrant, about 1 minute.

Add the greens, stock, chili flakes, and liquid smoke to the stockpot and bring to a boil.

Reduce heat, cover, and simmer for 35 to 40 minutes.

Allow greens to cool, then transfer them to a large bowl or Pyrex dish with a lid. Let the greens sit for 1 to 2 hours or overnight in the refrigerator. The overnight method is preferred to really let the flavors shine. Reheat on the stove and serve.

grilled vegetables

The great thing about fresh vegetables is that they are so darn cheap! Grilling vegetables turns them from being just another item on the plate to a chic main attraction. You can use almost any type of grill for this recipe. An outdoor or indoor grill, or even a panini press will get the job done.

¼ cup extra virgin olive oil

1 medium zucchini, sliced thin lengthwise

1 medium yellow summer squash, sliced thin lengthwise

6 spears asparagus, ends trimmed about 1 inch

1 tablespoon fresh rosemary

1 tablespoon fresh thyme

Freshly ground black pepper to taste

Sea salt to taste

Drizzle a large casserole dish with olive oil, lay vegetables flat, and drizzle with a little more olive oil. Sprinkle with rosemary, thyme, salt, and pepper and marinate for at least 30 minutes in the refrigerator.

Set your grill to high and fit as many veggies on the grill as possible. Grill for 3 to 5 minutes on both sides, making sure you're getting those beautiful grill marks. Turn the heat down to medium-high if your veggies start cooking a little too quickly.

MAKES 4 TO 6 SERVINGS

QUICK AND EASY
MEAL IDEAS:
SPAGHETTI WHO?
(PAGE 45) AND
FRUGAL FEAST
(PAGE 45)

COOK'S TIP:

If fresh herbs just aren't in the budget, feel free to use dried instead. Marinate the dried herbs in olive oil for at least 10 minutes to help bring out the flavor.

Steamed vegetables

MAKES 4 SERVINGS

QUICK AND EASY
MEAL IDEAS:
ITALIAN SIMPLICITY
(PAGE 46),
CHINESE TAKE-IN
(PAGE 46),
AND PUMPKIN PECAN
PERFECTION (PAGE 47)

This recipe is about as quick and easy as they come. You don't need a fancy steamer, just a metal steam basket, which usually costs no more than $4 and fits in any size pot. Add a little water to the pot, place the steam basket inside, and add your vegetables. Within 3 to 5 minutes you'll have perfectly steamed vegetables. Flax oil is a healthy substitute for margarine and a great way to add essential fatty acids to your diet.

1 pound fresh or frozen vegetables
¼ cup flax oil
Sea salt
Freshly ground black pepper to taste

Steam the vegetables until they are just tender. Transfer veggies to a large bowl and toss with oil.

Transfer to serving plate and add sea salt and pepper as desired.

easy oven-baked fries

I always wondered why, when I turned over a bag of frozen fries and checked the ingredient list, it was at least five lines long. Few things are easier to make than fries. You don't need much more than potatoes, seasoning, and a little oil to make great-tasting, better-for-you fries right at home.

3 large russet potatoes, scrubbed and cut into ¼- to ½-inch-thick strips
1½ tablespoons canola oil
1 tablespoon Old Bay Seasoning, or to taste

Preheat the oven to 350° F.

In a large bowl, toss the potatoes with oil and then Old Bay Seasoning.

Cover a baking sheet with foil and lightly oil the foil. Arrange the potatoes on the baking sheet in a single layer. Bake for 45 minutes or until golden brown and crispy.

MAKES 4 TO 6 SERVINGS

QUICK AND EASY
MEAL IDEAS:
THE STEAK DINNER
(PAGE 45), GAME DAY
(PAGE 46), AND
GIVE ME THAT FISH
(PAGE 46)

mac and cheeze

MAKES 6 TO 8 SERVINGS

QUICK AND EASY
MEAL IDEA:
SOUTHERN FRIED SPECIAL
(PAGE 45)

Mac and cheese is classic American comfort food. Nearly every-body has had mac and cheese once in their life. Whether it comes in a box or it's made from your great-grandmother's recipe handed down through the generations, there isn't another dish out there that screams classic American comfort food like mac and cheese. The vegan community has a special obsession with mac and cheese. If you do a Google search you will find hundreds of different recipes, some soy-based, some with nutritional yeast, some with margarine, some with oil, some baked, some made on the stovetop—the list goes on and on. I humbly lend my version to this tradition.

1 pound elbow macaroni or rotini pasta

2 medium Yukon Gold potatoes, peeled and diced

1 medium carrot, peeled and diced

⅔ cup diced white or yellow onion

2½ cups water

⅔ cups canola oil

⅓ cup raw cashews

⅓ cup macadamia nuts

2 teaspoons sea salt

2 garlic cloves, chopped

¼ teaspoon dry mustard

2 tablespoons fresh lemon juice

½ teaspoon pepper

¼ teaspoon cayenne pepper

¼ cup plain bread crumbs, optional

Sᴡᴇᴇᴛ Pᴏᴛᴀᴛᴏ Wᴀғғʟᴇs (ᴘᴀɢᴇ 52)
ᴀɴᴅ Sᴘɪɴᴀᴄʜ Oᴍᴇʟᴇᴛ (ᴘᴀɢᴇ 70)

Sloppy Josephs
(page 144)

Fool Your
Friends Tacos
(page 136)

Veggie "Meat" Loaf (page 173) with Smashed Potatoes (page 88) and Garlic Green Beans (page 86)

SPICY
PUMPKIN
SOUP
(PAGE 111)

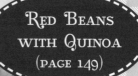

RED BEANS
WITH QUINOA
(PAGE 149)

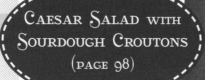

CAESAR SALAD WITH
SOURDOUGH CROUTONS
(PAGE 98)

"Pepperoni"
Mini Pizza
(and variations)
(page 151)

Tuno Tempeh Sandwich (page 168)

Peach Cobbler (page 210)

Preheat oven to 350° F.

Lightly oil a 3-quart casserole dish or six 6-ounce ramekins placed on a baking sheet.

Prepare the pasta according to package directions. Drain and set aside.

While pasta is cooking, combine the potatoes, carrots, onion, and 2½ cups water in a small saucepan and set over medium heat. Bring to a boil, turn down the heat until the water is simmering, and cook, covered, for 10 minutes or until the vegetables are tender. The smaller you cut the vegetables, the less time it will take to cook them.

Put the oil, cashews, macadamia nuts, salt, garlic, dry mustard, lemon juice, black pepper, cayenne, and cooked vegetables with the cooking water into a blender and process until completely smooth.

Toss cooked pasta with blended cheeze sauce until it is completely coated. Transfer the mixture to the casserole dish or ramekins, and sprinkle with bread crumbs, if using. Bake for 30 minutes or until the cheeze sauce is bubbling.

Cook's Tip:

If you do not have a high-speed blender use ⅔ cup cashews instead of the cashew and macadamia nuts mix, as cashews are softer and easier to process.

garlic green beans

QUICK AND EASY
MEAL IDEAS:
THE MEAN BEAN
(PAGE 42) AND
MAMA'S HOME COOKING
(PAGE 44)

Feel free to substitute fresh baby spinach for haricots verts in this dish. Follow the instructions, using 1 pound of fresh uncooked baby spinach, upping the olive oil to 3 tablespoons, and forgoing the almonds.

¼ cup slice white onion

1½ tablespoons extra virgin olive oil

3 garlic cloves, minced

10 ounces haricots verts or green beans, steamed

¼ cup slivered almonds, optional

Freshly ground black pepper to taste

Sea salt

Over medium heat, sauté the onion in olive oil for 2 minutes. Add the garlic and cook for an additional 1 minute. Add the haricots verts and sauté for 2 minutes.

If you are using almonds, add the almonds and cook an additional 1 minute. Remove from heat. Add salt and pepper to taste.

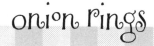
onion rings

I love onions! Sure, they might make your breath a little stinky, but that's why this recipe makes enough onion rings to feed four. Two people with onion breath cancel each other out, and when there are four people with onion breath, then you have pure onion ring bliss.

1 cup plain soy milk or oat milk

1 tablespoon arrowroot

1 tablespoon vegan Worcestershire sauce

1 cup unbleached all-purpose flour

1½ tablespoons Old Bay Seasoning

1 medium yellow onion, peeled and cut into ¼-inch-thick rings

Peanut or canola oil

QUICK AND EASY
MEAL IDEA:
BACKYARD BBQ
(PAGE 45) AND
THE HAMBURGER HALL
OF FAME (PAGE 47)

Whisk the milk, arrowroot, and Worcestershire sauce in a shallow bowl.

Combine the flour and Old Bay Seasoning in a separate shallow bowl or pan.

Dip the onions, one ring at a time, into the flour, then into the milk mixture, and back into the flour.

Heat the oil in a deep-fryer to 375° F or in a large skillet or frying pan over medium-high heat.

Fry onions in small batches until golden. Drain on a paper towel.

smashed potatoes

MAKES 4 SERVINGS

QUICK AND EASY
MEAL IDEA:
MAMA'S HOME COOKING
(PAGE 44)

Mashed potatoes are great and all, but they are so pretentious! They are like the time-consuming snobs of the potato world. You have to peel the potatoes, boil them, and then whip them into this perfect, fluffy, lump-free dollop. I personally like the lumps in mashed potatoes and hate adding extra steps where they aren't necessary. Smashed Potatoes are far from pretentious—just boil, mash, and serve.

5 medium new or red potatoes, skins on and cubed
¼ cup plain soy milk
Sea salt
Freshly ground black pepper to taste

Put the potatoes into a medium stockpot with just enough water to cover them by 1 inch. Bring to a boil over high heat and cook the potatoes until tender.

Allow the potatoes to cool and mash them with the back of a large spoon or a potato masher.

Add the soy milk and continue to mash until completely incorporated. Add salt and pepper to taste.

Spicy Corn

Corn is such a versatile grain. Yes, I said grain, not vegetable! Corn is not a vegetable but is actually an incredibly multitalented grain. You can find it in everything from soda pop (as high fructose corn syrup), which is anything but wholesome, to taco shells. Nowadays corn has been turned into a lot of things that are nutritionally appalling, but nothing can beat fresh, wholesome, whole-grain corn. So every once in a while you can live on the wild side and pretend that corn is a vegetable, too, and when you do, you have to make this delicious, spicy side dish.

One 10-ounce bag frozen corn
½ cup diced green bell pepper
¼ cup diced red or Spanish onion
1 teaspoon crushed red pepper flakes
½ cup vegetable stock

Mix all ingredients in a medium saucepan and simmer, covered, for 20 minutes. Serve warm.

MAKES 4 SERVINGS

QUICK AND EASY
MEAL IDEA:
BAJA CALIFORNIA DINNER
(PAGE 44)
AND ENCHILADA FIESTA
(PAGE 46)

classic cornbread

MAKES 4 TO 6 SERVINGS

QUICK AND EASY
MEAL IDEA:
SOUTHERN NIGHTS
(PAGE 44)

COOK'S TIP:

You can combine the dry ingredients ahead of time, store the mixture in an airtight container, and then just add the wet ingredients when you are ready to make a batch of cornbread. It's like having your own box of cornbread mix, but without all the preservatives and hidden animal parts.

Cornbread is one of the greatest breads ever invented. You can use it to sop up the juices from your collard greens or unashamedly wipe up the last bits of gravy from your plate, or pile it with mounds of Down-home Chili (page 129) for a savory, spicy, super-sloppy, satisfying meal.

My mother used to make cornbread in an old cast-iron skillet but if you don't have one handy, a 1½-quart casserole dish will work just fine.

¼ cup canola oil plus more for the pan

1 cup coarse cornmeal

1 cup unbleached all-purpose flour

2 tablespoons sugar

1 tablespoon plus 1 teaspoon baking powder

¾ teaspoon sea salt

2 tablespoons white vinegar

1¼ cup plain oat milk or soy milk

Preheat the oven to 425°F. Oil a cast-iron skillet or a 1½-quart casserole dish.

Mix the cornmeal, flour, sugar, baking powder, and salt until thoroughly combined. Create a well in the center and pour in the oil, vinegar, and oat milk. Mix until there are no lumps left and transfer to the skillet or baking dish.

Bake for 20 minutes or until a toothpick comes out clean.

vegetable tempura

I have a special love for vegetable tempura. Let's face it, every-thing is good battered and fried. I'm sure this book would be de-licious battered and fried. There's no question that, before long, you'll have a special love for vegetable tempura, too.

1½ cups cold water

1 ¼ cup unbleached all-purpose flour or white rice flour

½ cup soft silken tofu, pureed in a blender or food processor

½ small yam, peeled and thinly sliced

½ cup fresh broccoli florets

2 shiitake mushrooms, stems removed and sliced thin

½ cup fresh green beans, trimmed

½ cup thinly sliced carrots

Vegetable oil for frying

Heat the oil in a large frying pan or deep fryer to 375° F.

In a shallow dish, whisk cold water, flour, and tofu until com-pletely combined.

Dip the vegetables one at a time into the batter and place in the hot oil. Fry until golden brown and then allow the vegeta-bles to drain on paper towels.

Serve warm with your favorite dipping sauce.

MAKES 4 SERVINGS

QUICK AND EASY
MEAL IDEA:
EAST MEETS WEST
(PAGE 47)

soups and salads

alphabet soup

QUICK AND EASY
MEAL IDEA:
THE ABCs OF LUNCH
(PAGE 41)

You're never too old for alphabet soup, but just in case you think you are, feel free to substitute small shell-shaped pasta in place of the alphabet-shaped pasta.

4 cups vegetable stock

One 6-ounce can tomato paste

1 teaspoon agave nectar

1 medium carrot, peeled and diced

1 new potato, scrubbed and diced

½ cup frozen peas

½ cup fresh or frozen corn

½ cup fresh or frozen green beans, cut into 1-inch pieces

⅓ cup alphabet-shaped pasta

Whisk the vegetable stock with the tomato paste in a medium saucepan over medium-high heat. Add the agave, carrot, potato, peas, corn, and green beans and bring to a boil.

Once the soup begins to boil, add the pasta, lower the heat, cover, and simmer until pasta is cooked and potatoes can be pierced through with a fork, about 20 minutes, stirring occasionally.

Serve warm.

black bean soup

This soup has large hearty chunks of tomatoes in it, but if you're just not a fan of tomatoes, you can add one more can of black beans and omit the tomatoes.

1 tablespoon canola oil

½ cup chopped Spanish onion

1 garlic clove, minced

Two 15-ounce cans black beans, drained and rinsed

One 14.5-ounce can diced tomatoes with juice

4 cups vegetable stock

1 bay leaf

1 teaspoon ground cumin

¼ teaspoon sea salt

¼ teaspoon pepper

1 tablespoon fresh lime juice

½ teaspoon cayenne pepper

¼ cup plus 2 tablespoons vegan sour cream

1 cup chopped fresh cilantro

MAKES 4 SERVINGS

QUICK AND EASY
MEAL IDEA:
BLACK BEAN BONANZA
(PAGE 45)

Heat the oil in a large saucepan over medium heat and sauté onion and garlic until garlic is tender, about 1 to 2 minutes.

Stir in the beans, tomatoes, vegetable stock, bay leaf, cumin, salt, and pepper. Bring to a boil. Reduce to a simmer and cook, covered, for 20 minutes, stirring occasionally.

Remove soup from the heat. Discard the bay leaf. Stir in the lime juice and cayenne. Serve immediately, garnished with sour cream and cilantro.

creamy black bean soup

MAKES 4 SERVINGS

QUICK AND EASY
MEAL IDEA:
THE LITTLE SIN
(PAGE 47)

I love black bean soup so much I had to make two recipes. I like this one because it's completely oil free and therefore has a lot less fat. Who could hate that! And of course minimal ingredients mean minimal cash out of your pocket. This recipe requires a little more knife work, but the fresh ingredients can't be beat.

1 small tomato, chopped

¼ cup chopped red onion

¼ cup chopped green bell pepper

Two 15-ounce cans black beans, drained and rinsed

2 cups vegetable stock

1 teaspoon vegan Worcestershire sauce

¼ cup loosely packed cilantro, torn

Put all of the ingredients into a large saucepan, except the cilantro, and bring to a boil over medium-high heat. Reduce heat and simmer, covered, for 15 minutes. Allow to cool for 3 to 4 minutes.

In a blender, puree half or all of the soup (depending on your desired consistency). Return to the saucepan and reheat. Ladle into serving bowls and garnish with cilantro.

green salad

Every salad doesn't have to be an event. Sometimes you just need a simple green side salad to round out your lunch or dinner. The toppings for this salad are all completely optional, so feel free to experiment with different sprouts, vegetables, nuts, and seeds to make your perfect salad.

MAKES 4 SERVINGS

QUICK AND EASY
MEAL IDEAS:
IS IT CHILI IN HERE?
(PAGE 42),
TUNO ME IS TO LOVE ME
(PAGE 42),
SOUP AND SALAD FULLY
LOADED (PAGE 43),
MOBILE PIZZERIA
(PAGE 43),
TOO HOT TO HANDLE
(PAGE 43),
ITALIANO CLASSICO
(PAGE 46),
AND TUNI-ROLE SUPPER
(PAGE 47)

2 heads romaine, green leaf, or red leaf lettuce
½ cup thinly sliced radishes
1 large carrot, cut into thin strips or ribbons
½ cup grape or cherry tomatoes, cut in half
1 cup broccoli, alfalfa, or clove sprouts
½ cup raw husked sunflower seeds

Chop lettuce into ½-inch strips. Add all ingredients to a large bowl and toss with desired salad dressing.

COOK'S TIP:

To get perfectly thin ribbons, shave the carrot with a vegetable peeler.

caesar salad with sourdough croutons

MAKES 4 SERVINGS

QUICK AND EASY MEAL IDEAS:
TOUR OF ITALY (PAGE 43) AND CIAO BELLA! (PAGE 44)

When I was growing up and my family went to a restaurant, you could expect two things: I was always going to order the fettuccine Alfredo and my brother was always going to order the Caesar salad. Never in my life have I ever seen a little boy get more joy out of a salad than he did. Something about the creaminess of the salad dressing mixed with the crunch of the croutons just made it perfect. Every year for his birthday his only request was to go to his favorite restaurant and order a huge Caesar salad. Now every year on his birthday, I make this Caesar salad in his honor.

SOURDOUGH CROUTONS:
  2 slices sourdough bread
  Nonhydrogenated margarine
  Garlic powder
  Sea salt

CAESAR DRESSING:
  ¼ cup lemon juice (about 1 large lemon)
  1 tablespoon whole-grain mustard
  1 teaspoon Dijon mustard
  2 garlic cloves, chopped
  3 tablespoons nutritional yeast
  1½ tablespoons capers
  ¼ teaspoon vegan Worcestershire sauce
  ¼ teaspoon sea salt
  ¼ teaspoon pepper
  ½ cup vegan mayonnaise
  ¼ cup flaxseed oil or extra virgin olive oil
  2 large heads romaine lettuce, washed, dried and chopped into thin slices
  Vegan Parmesan cheese, optional

98   QUICK AND EASY VEGAN COMFORT FOOD

To make the Sourdough Croutons:

Spread each slice of bread with margarine. Dust garlic powder over bread and then sprinkle with a pinch of sea salt. If using a toaster oven, toast the bread on a medium or broil setting until the bread is toasted. Be careful to make sure that the garlic powder does not burn. If you are using an oven, put the bread under the broiler for a little less than a minute, watching closely to make sure it doesn't burn.

Allow to slightly cool and cut into ½-inch squares.

To make the Caesar Dressing:

Blend all the ingredients, except oil, in a blender until the mixture is a creamy consistency.

Turn the blender down to the lowest level and slowly add the oil until well incorporated.

Assemble the salad:

Transfer the lettuce to a large bowl and add Caesar Dressing two tablespoons at a time, incorporating with a spatula, until every leaf is covered with dressing (but not drenched).

Transfer the salad to serving plates, top with Sourdough Croutons, and sprinkle with vegan Parmesan cheese, if using, and freshly ground pepper.

french onion soup

MAKES 4 SERVINGS

QUICK AND EASY
MEAL IDEA:
BACKPACKING THROUGH
EUROPE (PAGE 46)

Ahhh, French onion soup, my favorite vegetarian mistake. I loved this so much in my omnivore days that I just assumed since it was an onion soup that it had to be vegetarian. Boy, was I wrong. I was just three months into being vegetarian when one of my coworkers informed me that French onion soup is made with beef broth! Imagine my horror, especially since I hadn't eaten beef in nearly a decade. But hey, we all make mistakes, and from that day forward the French onion soup and I parted ways. But now here we are, reunited . . . and it feels so good (sing along!).

¼ cup nonhydrogenated margarine

3 medium white or yellow onions, thinly sliced

3 garlic cloves, thinly sliced

1 teaspoon sugar

Dash of pepper

2 tablespoon unbleached all-purpose flour

5½ cups vegetable stock

½ cup red wine or dry sherry wine

1 tablespoon vegan Worcestershire sauce

2 teaspoons fresh thyme

1 French baguette

Vegan mozzarella, sliced thin

Preheat the oven to 450° F.

Melt the margarine in a large Dutch oven or stockpot. Add the onions and cook over medium-low heat for 25 minutes or until soft and caramelized, stirring often. About 15 minutes into cooking the onions add the garlic, sugar, and pepper.

When the onions are caramelized, stir in the flour until well blended. Stir in the vegetable stock, wine, Worcestershire sauce, and thyme. Bring the soup to a boil. Reduce heat to low, cover, and simmer for 10 minutes.

Cut four 1-inch slices of baguette and toast until just lightly brown.

Place four ovenproof bowls on a foil-covered baking sheet and ladle in the soup. Place 1 toasted baguette slice on top of each bowl of soup and cover with mozzarella.

Bake for 10 minutes or just until cheese has begun to melt. Conversely, you can also place the soup under the broiler until cheese has melted, about 1 or 2 minutes.

coconut corn chowder

MAKES 4 SERVINGS

QUICK AND EASY
MEAL IDEA:
A CORNY LUNCH
(PAGE 44)

In the sticky-hot Georgia summer, the last thing you need is something to raise your body temperature one more degree. So I try to stay away from soups in the summer, but this soup is my rare exception to the rule. In the summer, my local co-op stocks white and yellow corn from local farms that make this soup sweet and delightful. If you don't have access to fresh, in-season corn, then 2 heaping cups of frozen corn can be substituted.

1 tablespoon canola oil

½ cup yellow onion, diced

½ large red bell pepper, diced

2 garlic cloves, minced

3 cups vegetable stock

¾ cups unsweetened coconut milk

1 tablespoon diced oil-packed sun-dried tomatoes

3 ears white corn, yellow corn, or a mix, corn cut from the cobs

1 avocado, diced

Pinch of sea salt

Freshly ground black pepper

Warm the oil over medium heat in a medium stockpot. Add the onion and cook until onions become somewhat translucent, about 2 to 3 minutes. Add the bell pepper and garlic and cook for an additional minute, stirring constantly.

Add the vegetable stock, coconut milk, tomatoes, corn, and salt and pepper to taste. Bring to a boil, reduce heat and simmer for 10 minutes.

Evenly distribute avocado among serving bowls and ladle soup on top. Serve warm.

fresh corn salad

Usually I'm pretty flexible on the use of fresh or frozen vegetables and grains, but for my fresh corn salad I have to emphasize the word "fresh." This salad is all about the texture and flavor of fresh summer corn. The longer you let it marinate in the refrigerator the bolder the flavor, so feel free to refrigerate it overnight if you have the time.

3 cups fresh, white corn kernels (approximately 4 ears corn)

1 medium tomato, seeded and chopped

½ cup diced red bell pepper

½ cup diced green bell pepper

½ cup finely diced red onion

Juice of 1 lime

1 jalapeño, minced, remove seeds if you desire less heat

1 tablespoon extra virgin olive oil or flax oil

Toss all ingredients together in a medium bowl, cover with plastic wrap or a tight-fitting lid, and let marinate in the refrigerator for at least an hour. Serve chilled.

MAKES 4 SERVINGS

QUICK AND EASY MEAL IDEA: CALIFORNIA FRESH MEX (PAGE 41), TOFU OF THE SEA (PAGE 44), TIJUANA TORPEDO (PAGE 45), AND A CORNY LUNCH (PAGE 44)

loaded baked potato soup

MAKES 4 SERVINGS

QUICK AND EASY
MEAL IDEA:
SOUP AND SALAD FULLY
LOADED (PAGE 43)

This soup is insanely easy and insanely good. It captures everything that is wonderful about a baked potato loaded up with vegan cheese, sour cream, chives, and vegan bacon bits. Don't feel restricted by the topping choices. After you try the recipe once as is, play with the toppings. You can add some thinly sliced and pan-fried Breakfast Sausage (page 50) or boost your intake of vegetables by adding steamed chopped broccoli or cauliflower.

2 medium russet potatoes, scrubbed

1 tablespoon canola oil, optional

2 cups vegetable stock

1 cup plain soy milk

¼ teaspoon hickory liquid smoke

⅛ teaspoon sea salt

¼ teaspoon pepper

½ cup shredded vegan cheddar or Cheezly mature white cheddar

¼ cup plus 2 tablespoons vegan sour cream

2 green onions, sliced, or 3 tablespoons fresh chives, snipped

2 tablespoons vegetarian bacon bits, optional

There are three ways to cook the potatoes: bake them, steam them, or microwave them. For all versions, scrub the skin of the potatoes to get off all the dirt.

For baked potatoes: Preheat the oven to 350° F. Rub 1 tablespoon of canola oil over the potatoes evenly and place them on a baking sheet lined with foil. Bake for 1 hour, until a knife meets no resistance. Let them cool, then cut the potatoes into medium pieces (about ½ inch square).

For steamed potatoes: Cut the potatoes into ½-inch-square pieces, place in a steamer over boiling water, and steam until tender, about 15 minutes.

For microwaved potatoes: Microwave the whole potatoes on high for 5 minutes, turning them over at the 2½-minute mark.

Allow potatoes to cool, then cut potatoes into medium pieces (about ½ inch square).

Combine the potatoes, stock, soy milk, liquid smoke, salt, and pepper, in a medium stockpot and bring to a low boil. Once the mixture begins to boil, lower the heat and simmer, covered, for 5 minutes. Watch closely to make sure the soup does not boil over, stirring occasionally.

Puree one-quarter to one-half of the potato mixture with an emulsion blender or regular blender. Add this back to the soup.

Remove soup from the heat and stir in ¼ cup vegan cheese, sour cream, and one of the green onions (or 1½ tablespoons of chives).

Use the remaining ingredients to garnish the soup, and serve warm.

hearty slow-cooked vegetable soup

MAKES 4 TO 6 SERVINGS

QUICK AND EASY
MEAL IDEA:
HONEY, I'M HOME!
(PAGE 48)

As a single girl it's my dream to come home to a home-cooked meal ready and waiting for me after a long day. I'm pretty sure this dream is shared by everyone on this earth who's single. Thanks to the slow-cooker, this dream is a reality.

I like to prep the vegetables the night before, then toss everything in the slow-cooker the next morning. Eight hours later I have the pleasure of walking into the house to the smell of warm, homemade soup.

1 garlic clove, minced

1 vegetable bouillon cube

One 1-ounce envelope vegan onion soup mix

2 medium russet potatoes or 4 red potatoes, chopped

5 cups water

One 14.5-ounce can diced tomatoes, with juices

1 cup fresh broccoli florets

1 cup chopped fresh cauliflower

1 cup chopped fresh carrots

1 cup fresh green beans, cut into 1-inch pieces

1 cup frozen peas

¼ teaspoon black pepper

Combine all the ingredients in a slow-cooker and cook for 4 hours on high or 8 hours on low. Serve warm.

COOK'S TIP:

The peas tend to cook really quickly, so, you can stir them in after the soup is finished cooking, if you like; the temperature of the soup will quickly cook the peas. This might lower the overall temperature of your soup, so allow time for the soup to heat up again before serving.

I get as giddy as a five-year-old whenever I'm invited out to a Japanese restaurant, because I know that where there is Japanese food there is sure to be miso soup. For so long, I thought that miso soup was just too good not to be somehow overly complicated to make. Then one day I noticed miso paste at the grocery store and my world became a happier place. As it turns out, miso soup is one of the quickest and easiest soups to make and yet it packs a ton of flavor.

MAKES 2 SERVINGS

QUICK AND EASY
MEAL IDEAS:
SOBA SIESTA (PAGE 42)
AND JAPANESE TAKEOUT
(PAGE 42)

- 1½ cups vegetable stock
- 1 green onion, white and green parts chopped
- 3 ounces firm silken tofu, diced
- 2 tablespoons dried wakame
- 1½ tablespoons white or red miso
- ½ cup water

Bring the stock, tofu, green onions, and wakame to a boil.

In a separate bowl, whisk the miso with water. Add the miso mixture to the soup and stir until combined. Simmer until soup is warmed through. Transfer to serving bowls and serve warm.

on-hand bean and pasta soup

MAKES 4 SERVINGS

QUICK AND EASY
MEAL IDEAS:
QUICK, FAST, AND IN A
HURRY (PAGE 47)

The name of this soup tells it all. Look in the cabinets, look in the refrigerator . . . take everything out and throw it in a stockpot. Voilà! You have soup.

½ cup roughly chopped white onion

1 medium carrot, peeled and chopped

2 tablespoons canola oil

1 garlic clove, minced

2½ cups vegetable stock

1 bay leaf

One 14.5-ounce can diced tomatoes, with juices

One 15-ounce can garbanzo beans, drained

¾ cup rotini pasta

Sauté the onion and carrots in the canola oil for 2 minutes. Add the garlic and sauté for an additional 2 minutes.

Add the stock, bay leaf, tomatoes, and garbanzo beans. Bring to a boil and add the pasta. Cook until pasta is al dente, 7 to 9 minutes. Discard the bay leaf and serve.

picnic pasta salad

MAKES 4 TO 6 SERVINGS

Except for one year in Philadelphia, I have always been fortunate to live in regions of the country where spring comes early. By the time the first of March rolls around, I have already dusted off my picnic basket and started planning a menu for my first spring outing to the park. Whether you welcome spring with a picnic or a backyard BBQ with friends, you must add this quick and easy pasta salad to your celebration.

QUICK AND EASY
MEAL IDEA:
THE LUNCH BOX
(PAGE 43)

1 pound pasta (elbow macaroni or rotini), cooked according to package directions

½ cup chopped celery

½ cup chopped red onion

1 cup vegan mayonnaise

1 teaspoon stone-ground mustard

1 teaspoon apple cider vinegar

½ cup sweet pickle relish

½ cup halved grape tomatoes

½ cup diced red bell pepper

2 teaspoons sugar

¼ teaspoon sea salt

Freshly ground pepper to taste

Combine cooled pasta with the rest of the ingredients in a large bowl. Refrigerate for at least an hour or overnight and serve chilled.

potato salad

QUICK AND EASY
MEAL IDEA:
DELI AT YOUR DESK
(PAGE 44)

Potato salad is a great year-round dish. It's a classic at a summer BBQ, one of many sides at Thanksgiving dinner, pushed next to the baked beans and corn on the cob on your flimsy paper plate at a party for the big football game in the winter, or an accompaniment to Fried Chik'n Seitan (page 139) for a springtime picnic at the park.

5 new potatoes, skin on and cubed

¼ cup diced red onions

¼ teaspoon mustard

¼ cup vegan mayonnaise

½ teaspoon sugar

3 tablespoons sweet relish

2 tablespoons diced celery

Paprika

Place the potatoes in a medium stockpot with a pinch of sea salt and enough water to cover them by an inch. Boil until tender, about 20 minutes. Drain potatoes and let cool completely.

Combine cooled potatoes with remaining ingredients, except paprika, in a large bowl. Transfer to a serving dish and sprinkle with paprika. Serve cold.

Spicy Pumpkin Soup

The longer you let this soup sit, the spicier it will get. So if you don't think you'll be eating all of this in one sitting, use half the amount of red pepper flakes you would normally use and when you reheat the soup add the other half. You can also substitute butternut squash or sweet potato puree in place of pumpkin.

2 cups pumpkin puree

One 14-ounce can unsweetened coconut milk

1 cup vegetable stock

3 tablespoons agave nectar

1 teaspoons red pepper flakes

Whisk the pumpkin puree, coconut milk, and vegetable stock in a medium stockpot.

Stir in the agave nectar and red pepper flakes. Bring to a low boil and simmer, covered, for 10 minutes. Serve warm.

MAKES 4 SERVINGS

QUICK AND EASY MEAL IDEA:
PUMPKIN PECAN PERFECTION (PAGE 47)

Sweet potato Soup

MAKES 4 SERVINGS

QUICK AND EASY
MEAL IDEA:
SOPHISTICATED SOUL
(PAGE 45)

Although canned, pureed sweet potatoes are more convenient, homemade mashed sweet potatoes really add a natural sweetness to this soup that you just can't get with canned sweet potatoes. To make mashed sweet potatoes, bake a large sweet potato/yam at 450° F until soft and the natural sugars start to bake out, about 45 minutes. Carefully cut open the potato. Spoon out the soft flesh and measure 1½ cups.

1 tablespoon unbleached all-purpose flour

1 tablespoon canola oil

1½ cups vegetable stock

2 tablespoons light brown sugar

1½ cups cooked mashed sweet potatoes or pureed sweet potatoes

¼ teaspoon ground ginger

¼ teaspoon ground cinnamon

¼ teaspoon grated nutmeg

1 cup plain soy milk or oat milk

Whisk the flour with the oil, and cook it over medium heat, stirring constantly, until it becomes a light caramel color. Whisk in the stock and brown sugar and bring it all to a boil.

Stir in the sweet potatoes and spices. Reduce heat, then lower to a simmer, cover, and cook 5 minutes more. Allow to cool. Puree the soup with an immersion blender or regular blender and return to the pot. If you are using pureed sweet potatoes, you can forgo the blender step.

Add the soy milk and reheat the soup. Serve warm.

tomato and avocado soup

While traveling in Costa Rica I came across a rich and luscious tomato soup with beautiful ripe avocado swimming in it at a small restaurant near the home I was staying at. I was shocked at what a great combination it was. When I returned to the States I immediately began work on recreating the soup. This is my version of the Costa Rican classic.

One 28-ounce can whole tomatoes with juices

½ cup plain soy milk or oat milk

1 small leek, cleaned and chopped

10 leaves fresh basil

1 tablespoon light brown sugar

⅛ teaspoon sea salt

¼ teaspoon pepper

½ cup vegetable stock (keep more on hand just in case)

½ medium ripe avocado, seeded and diced

Combine the tomatoes, their juices, soy milk, leek, basil, brown sugar, salt, and pepper in a food processor or blender. Pulse until thoroughly combined. Slowly add the vegetable stock until your desired consistency is reached.

Transfer the soup into a medium saucepan and warm over medium heat for 15 minutes.

Divide the avocado pieces evenly in four bowls, ladle soup into each bowl, and serve hot.

MAKES 4 SERVINGS

QUICK AND EASY
MEAL IDEA:
AVOCADO MADNESS
(PAGE 41)

tortilla soup

MAKES 4 SERVINGS

QUICK AND EASY
MEAL IDEA:
TORTILLA SQUARED
(PAGE 43)

Tortilla Soup is real California comfort food. When I was working on this recipe I was surprised at how many omnivores doubted that it was possible to make a traditional tortilla soup without chicken or any type of chicken analog. Much to their surprise, I was able to make a vegan tortilla soup that is arguably better than the meat-laden version.

One 6-ounce can tomato paste

½ cup plain soy milk or oat milk

3 cups vegetable stock

One 14.5-ounce can diced tomatoes, with juices

1 or 2 chipotle peppers in adobo sauce, minced

½ cup diced Spanish onions

½ cup diced celery

1 cup fresh or frozen corn

2 garlic cloves, minced

¼ teaspoon chili powder

Sea salt

Freshly ground pepper to taste

Crushed tortilla chips

½ cup cilantro, torn

½ avocado, diced

Whisk the tomato paste with the soy milk in a medium stockpot until completely combined. Add the stock, tomatoes, their juices, chipotles, onions, celery, corn, garlic, chili powder, and salt and pepper to taste. Bring to a boil, lower heat, cover, and simmer for 10 minutes.

Ladle into four serving bowls and garnish with crushed tortilla chips, cilantro, and avocado.

winter bean soup

I love soup. It's like a warm blanket that covers you on a chilly day. When I'm on the road I make sure to carry a thermos of this soup to warm me up wherever I go. Pureed cannellini beans give this soup its thick and creamy consistency that sticks to your ribs and is sure to warm you up on cold winter days.

1 large carrot, peeled and diced

1 tablespoon canola oil

½ cup diced celery

½ leek, diced (1 inch of green parts included)

1 garlic clove, minced

3½ cups vegetable stock

Two 15-ounce cans cannellini beans (white kidney beans), drained and rinsed

1 cup fresh or frozen corn

1 bay leaf

⅛ teaspoon sea salt

¼ teaspoon pepper

Extra virgin olive oil or flax oil, optional

Sauté the carrots in oil in a large stockpot for 3 minutes. Add the celery, leeks, and garlic, and cook for an additional 2 minutes.

Add the stock, beans, corn, bay leaf, salt, and pepper. Bring to a boil, reduce heat, and simmer for 15 minutes.

Remove soup from the heat and cool for 5 minutes. Remove the bay leaf. Transfer half of the soup to a blender and blend until smooth (or use an immersion blender and blend until it reaches a consistency you like). Add the blended soup back to the stockpot and bring the soup back up to simmer over low heat until warm.

Ladle soup into four bowls and drizzle with a little extra virgin olive oil or flax oil, if desired. Serve warm.

MAKES 4 SERVINGS

QUICK AND EASY
MEAL IDEA:
A LASAGNA YOU CAN'T
REFUSE (PAGE 47)

taco salad

MAKES 2 SALADS

QUICK AND EASY
MEAL IDEAS:
ALL-N-ONE (PAGE 43)

The shell of this salad is, to me, the most important part of the whole recipe. You can make your own but I recommend finding a light, fluffy store-bought version. My personal favorite is Azteca brand taco salad shells. You can find them in the dairy section of your local grocery store, usually near the premade biscuits and cookies. If you can't find the premade taco salad shells, don't stress it. Making your own is a quick and easy process—just follow the instructions below.

1 cup vegetable stock

1½ teaspoons hickory liquid smoke

1 cup textured vegetable protein (TVP)

1 tablespoon canola oil

2 tablespoons Taco Seasoning Mix (page 201)

1 tablespoon water

2 large flour tortillas

2 cups refried beans

⅔ cups shredded lettuce

½ cup Chunky Fresh Salsa Picada (page 194) or Pico de Gallo (page 199)

¼ cup shredded vegan cheddar, optional

2 tablespoons vegan sour cream

1 green onion, sliced

Bring the stock and liquid smoke to a boil in a small pot. Add the TVP and let sit for 5 minutes.

Warm the oil in a medium skillet over medium heat. Add rehydrated TVP, Taco Seasoning, and water. Cook until all the water has been absorbed.

To make the Taco Salad shells:

Preheat the oven to 375° F.

Lightly oil each tortilla on both sides. Drape tortillas over small ovenproof bowls or over clean, empty tin cans (the can from the refried beans is a perfect fit). Bake for 2 or 3 minutes or until shells become golden brown.

Layer all ingredients in the two premade or homemade taco salad shells in the following order: refried beans, rehydrated TVP, lettuce, salsa, cheddar, sour cream, and green onions.

main courses

avocado melt panini

MAKES 2 SERVINGS

Quick and Easy
Meal Idea:
Avocado Madness
(page 41)

This is everything you love about guacamole, stuck between two pieces of sourdough, and layered with cheese. It doesn't get much better than this.

4 slices sourdough bread

8 slices meltable vegan mozzarella

1 avocado, mashed

1 slice red onion ring, halved

1 Roma tomato, sliced thin

½ cup cilantro, chopped

Extra virgin olive oil

Layer each slice of bread with 2 slices of mozzarella. Evenly distribute the mashed avocado, onion, tomato, and cilantro on two of the slices of bread.

Close the sandwiches and lightly drizzle the outside with olive oil. Grill on a panini press for 5 minutes or until mozzarella is completely melted.

avocado sandwich with dill sauce

MAKES 4 SANDWICHES

QUICK AND EASY
MEAL IDEA:
DILL OR NO DILL
(PAGE 42)

It's hard to believe, but there was once a time when the avocado was the villain behind every diet craze. Although the average avocado does contain 30 grams of fat, most of it is monounsaturated, meaning it is the "good" fat that actually helps lower cholesterol. As if that were not enough, avocado contains a phytonutrient called beta-sitosterol that has also been shown to help lower cholesterol. Many experts now recommend avocado as part of a healthy, balanced diet. This sandwich puts all the talents of avocado on display, front and center.

DILL SAUCE:

¼ cup vegan mayonnaise

¼ cup vegan sour cream

¼ cup fresh dill, chopped

8 slices multigrain, whole wheat, or whole spelt bread

½ medium green bell pepper, cut into thin strips

½ small red onion, sliced thin

½ tomato, sliced thin

One 3-ounce container sunflower sprouts

2 avocados, sliced into at least 4 strips per side

To make the Dill Sauce:

Stir together the mayonnaise and sour cream. Stir in chopped dill until thoroughly combined.

To make the sandwiches:

Lay out slices of bread, spread each slice with Dill Sauce and layer the rest of the ingredients as you like.

ultimate grilled cheeze

MAKES 4 SANDWICHES

QUICK AND EASY
MEAL IDEA:
THE ABCs OF LUNCH
(PAGE 41)

Summer comes early in my hometown of Fresno, California. By April, temperatures are already starting to creep up into the nineties, making it unbearable to stand in a hot kitchen any longer than absolutely necessary. After walking a mile home from school, with a heavy backpack on in the midst of one of these hot spring days, a grilled cheese sandwich was the quickest and easiest thing to make before it was time to start my homework. A decade later I much prefer this grown-up version of grilled cheese with Garlic Herb Spread (page 189) and tomato. You can even add broccoli, alfalfa, or clover sprouts to this sandwich to give it a bit of a nutrient boost.

1 recipe Garlic Herb Spread (page 189)
4 slices meltable vegan mozzarella
8 slices sourdough bread
½ medium tomato, sliced thin

Liberally slather Garlic Herb Spread on each slice of bread. Top with mozzarella and tomato. Close the sandwiches and grill with a panini press until the cheese begins to melt.

baked ziti

It's no wonder that baked ziti is a universal comfort food. The ingredients are minimal and are pantry standards. It's incredibly cheap to make, delicious, and it fills you up. What more could you want?

Canola oil for the casserole dish

1 cup vegetable stock

1½ teaspoons hickory liquid smoke

1 cup textured vegetable protein (TVP)

1 pound ziti, cooked according to package directions

½ cup diced onion

3 garlic cloves, minced

4 cups marinara sauce

½ cup vegetable stock

⅛ teaspoon sea salt

¼ teaspoon pepper

2 cups shredded vegan meltable mozzarella

Preheat the oven to 350°F. Oil a 3-quart casserole dish.

Bring the stock and liquid smoke to a boil in a small pot. Add the TVP and let sit for 5 minutes.

Combine the prepared TVP, cooked pasta, onion, garlic, marinara sauce, stock, salt, and pepper in a large bowl.

Put half of the pasta mixture into the casserole dish. Sprinkle with 1 cup of mozzarella. Add the remaining pasta, and top with the remaining mozzarella.

Cover with foil and bake for 20 minutes. Remove the foil and bake for an additional 10 minutes. If the cheese has not melted to your liking, put the dish under a broiler until the cheese completely melts, about 1 minute.

MAKES 4 TO 6 SERVINGS

QUICK AND EASY
MEAL IDEA:
FRUGAL FEAST
(PAGE 45)

COOK'S TIP:

If you don't have ziti on hand, you can use penne, rotini, or fusilli instead.

ultimate nachos

I can't decide what I love more, doctoring up store-bought vegan cheese to top these ultimate nachos or whipping up some of my own homemade Nacho Cheeze Sauce (page 198). If your local health food or grocery store carries meltable vegan cheese, then I recommend trying the recipe both ways—once with homemade Nacho Cheeze Sauce and once with the doctored-up store-bought variety. Either way, you're sure to be licking your fingers, and possibly the plate, after trying these nachos.

Canola oil spray for the baking dish

9 or 10 ounces tortilla chips

1 cup vegan meltable cheddar, shredded

¼ cup plain soy milk

1 cup shredded vegan meltable Monterey Jack, shredded

1 cup cooked black beans

½ cup diced bell pepper, any color

½ medium jalapeño, diced, optional

3 green onions, chopped

½ medium tomato, chopped

Preheat the oven to 450° F.

Spray a large (3-quart) baking dish with canola oil. Line the bottom of the casserole dish with tortilla chips.

Warm the cheddar and soy milk in a small saucepan over medium heat. Stir frequently until the cheese has melted.

Pour the cheddar mixture evenly over the chips. Sprinkle Monterey Jack over the cheddar.

Top with the beans, bell pepper, and jalapeño, if using. Bake for 5 to 7 minutes.

Remove from the oven, top with green onions and tomato, and serve.

bbq nachos

*South meets Southwest in this sinfully delicious take on nachos.
This is not a dish you want to make for date night or when you
are entertaining anyone you care to impress. There's no cute way
to eat these nachos, you just have to dive in and go for it—both
hands. Don't worry if it gets all over your mouth, if your fingers
are covered in BBQ Sauce, or even if you end up with a little bit
of TVP on your shirt. That's what washing machines and napkins
were made for, after all.*

9 or 10 ounces tortilla chips

1 cup vegetable stock

1½ teaspoons hickory liquid smoke

1 tablespoon vegan Worcestershire sauce

1 cup textured vegetable protein (TVP)

2 cups shredded vegan meltable Monterey Jack

1 chipotle pepper in adobo sauce, minced

¼ cup soy milk

1¼ cups BBQ Sauce (page 190)

Pour the tortilla chips into a large (3-quart) baking dish.

Bring the stock, liquid smoke, and Worcestershire sauce to a
boil and add the TVP. Turn off the heat, and let stand for 5 minutes, then fluff with a fork. Set aside.

Put the Monterey Jack, chipotle pepper, and soy milk into a
small saucepan and warm over medium heat. Stir frequently
until the cheese has melted.

Pour the cheese mixture over the tortilla chips.

Stir together the rehydrated TVP and the BBQ Sauce. Top the
nachos with the TVP mixture and serve.

cheeze enchiladas

MAKES 10 ENCHILADAS

QUICK AND EASY
MEAL IDEA:
BLACK BEAN BONANZA
(PAGE 45) AND ENCHI-
LADA FIESTA (PAGE 46)

In my hometown of Fresno, California, there is an incredible Mexican restaurant called Ole Frijole. I could eat a dozen of their cheese enchiladas and still come running back for more. I only make it home about once a year these days, and, as you might imagine, Ole Frijole doesn't make vegan enchiladas. But their cheese enchiladas have a taste I could never forget and that was surprisingly easy to translate into a vegan version. Because the cheese is not the highlight of these enchiladas you can use all Monterey Jack if you'd like, but not all cheddar.

24 ounces Enchilada Sauce (page 194)

¼ cup diced white, yellow, or Spanish onion

2 cups shredded vegan meltable cheddar

2 cups shredded vegan meltable Monterey Jack

1 tablespoon diced canned green chilies, or more, to taste

Ten 5-inch corn tortillas

Preheat the oven to 450° F.

Lightly oil a 2- to 2½-quart casserole dish. Coat the bottom of the dish with Enchilada Sauce.

Combine the onions, 1½ cups cheddar, 1cup Monterey Jack, and chilies in a medium bowl.

Heat the tortillas, five at a time, for 30 seconds in microwave to soften.

Fill each tortilla evenly with the cheese mixture; roll and place seam side down in the cooking dish.

When all the enchiladas have been assembled, pour the remaining Enchilada Sauce over them and sprinkle the remaining cheese evenly over them as well.

Bake for 15 minutes covered with foil. Remove the foil and bake for another 10 minutes. If the cheese has not completely melted, put the enchiladas under the broiler for 1 to 2 minutes, watching carefully to make sure they don't burn.

Variations

Black Bean Enchiladas

Replace ½ cup cheddar and ¼ cup Monterey Jack in the filling with ¾ cup cooked black beans (canned are fine) and ¼ cup fresh or frozen corn (do not thaw). Follow the rest of the recipe as is.

Vegetable Enchiladas

Replace ½ cup cheddar cheese and ¼ cup Monterey Jack in the filling with ⅓ cup fresh or frozen corn, ⅓ cup diced zucchini, ⅓ cup diced summer squash, and 2 tablespoons chopped cilantro. Follow the rest of the recipe as is.

Chik'n Enchiladas

Replace ½ cup cheddar and ¼ cup Monterey Jack with 1 cup shredded mock chicken (Chik'n Seitan [page 138] or store-bought mock chicken strips). To give the mock chicken a shredded look, pulse it 2 or 3 times in a food processor or roughly chop. Follow the rest of the recipe as is.

enchiladas sin queso

MAKES 10 ENCHILADAS

QUICK AND EASY
MEAL IDEA:
SAY QUESO!
(PAGE 48)

The first time I made vegetable enchiladas for my mom she kept going on and on about how they would be just fine without the cheese, so Mom, this one is for you.

¼ cup finally chopped white or Spanish onion

2 tablespoons canned diced green chilies

2 cup cooked black beans

½ cup fresh or frozen corn (do not thaw)

½ cup zucchini, diced

½ cup summer squash, diced

¼ cup cilantro, roughly chopped

24 to 30 ounces Enchilada Sauce (page 193)

Ten 5 inch corn tortillas

Preheat oven to 450° F.

Lightly oil a 2- to 2 ½- quart casserole dish and then cover entire bottom of cooking dish with Enchilada Sauce, just until coated.

Combine onions, green chilies, black beans, corn, zucchini, squash, cilantro, and 6 ounces of Enchilada Sauce in a medium bowl.

Heat tortillas, five at a time, for 30 seconds in microwave to soften.

Fill each tortilla evenly with bean/vegetable mixture, roll, and place seam side down in cooking dish.

When all enchiladas have been assembled, pour remaining Enchilada Sauce over them.

Bake for 25 minutes covered with foil.

down-home chili

With a well-stocked pantry, you can't go wrong with this recipe. The key to canned beans is to buy organic and buy on sale. They last for at least a year, so stock up! As for the spices, try to buy them from bulk bins, as they are always cheaper and you can buy exactly the amount you need.

One 14-ounce can kidney beans, drained and rinsed

One 14-ounce can pinto beans, drained and rinsed

One 28-ounce can diced tomatoes, with juices

¼ cup water

1 teaspoon ground cumin

1 teaspoon paprika

1½ tablespoons chili powder

1 teaspoon dried oregano

½ teaspoon sea salt

¼ teaspoon pepper

1 teaspoon onion powder

1 teaspoon garlic powder

⅛ teaspoon cayenne pepper

½ teaspoon allspice

Combine the beans, diced tomatoes with juices, water, and all the herbs and spices in a medium saucepan over medium-high heat until the mixture begins to bubble.

Lower the heat and simmer on low for 15 minutes.

Serve warm.

MAKES 4 SERVINGS

QUICK AND EASY
MEAL IDEA:
IS IT CHILI IN HERE?
(PAGE 42)

fettuccine alfredo two ways

MAKES 4 SERVINGS

QUICK AND EASY
MEAL IDEA:
BACKPACKING THROUGH
EUROPE (PAGE 46)

From my first bite of fettuccine Alfredo, I was hooked. For me, it is the epitome of comfort food—rich, creamy, buttery, and delicious. When I was in college I always kept a jar of premade Alfredo sauce on standby in the refrigerator. All I had to do was heat it up, toss in some pasta and steamed broccoli, and I was in heaven. I love fettuccine Alfredo so much that I created not one but two recipes. Although they use very different ingredients, both sauces have the same rich, velvety texture and taste. Sauce One is perfect for those days when you come home exhausted and just don't have the time or willpower to make a complicated meal. Sauce Two is an ideal weekend recipe, when you have 15 or 20 minutes to spare.

SAUCE ONE:

12.3 ounces soft silken tofu

½ cup canola oil

½ teaspoon onion powder

¼ cup nutritional yeast

1 teaspoon sea salt, or more, to taste

2 garlic cloves, chopped

Freshly ground black pepper to taste

SAUCE TWO:

½ cup nonhydrogenated margarine

2 garlic cloves, minced

1½ cups plain soy milk creamer (or other nondairy creamer)

1½ tablespoons arrowroot

2 tablespoons vegan cream cheese

Sea salt to taste

Freshly ground pepper to taste

½ pound (8 ounces) fettuccine, cooked according to package directions

To make Sauce One:

Put all the ingredients except the pepper in a blender and puree until smooth. Transfer to a small saucepan and warm the sauce over medium heat.

To make Sauce Two:

Melt the margarine in a medium saucepan over medium heat. Add the garlic and cook for 1 minute. Slowly stir in 1 cup soy milk creamer and bring to a low boil.

In a small bowl, whisk the remaining ½ cup of soy milk creamer with the arrowroot. Whisk this into the sauce. Then whisk the cream cheese into the sauce and continue a low boil just long enough to warm through, about 2 to 3 minutes.

Divide the fettuccine among four serving plates, ladle the sauce over the pasta, and top with freshly ground black pepper and sea salt.

dilla

MAKES 4 SERVINGS

QUICK AND EASY
MEAL IDEA:
THE LUNCH BOX
(PAGE 43)

Well . . . I would call it a quesadilla, but there's no queso in this Dilla. Queso or no queso, it's still amazing.

1 cup Plain Ol' Hummus (page 183)
¼ cup cilantro, chopped
Four 8- or 12-inch flour tortillas
½ medium tomato, sliced thin
½ small red onion, sliced thin
1 cup baby spinach
2 tablespoons canola oil

Stir together the hummus and chopped cilantro.

Lay out 4 tortillas. Spread the hummus mixture evenly among one half of each tortilla. On the same side, layer on the tomato, onion, and spinach. Fold the empty half of the tortilla over.

In a large skillet, warm 1 tablespoon of canola oil. Place two Dillas in the skillet and cook until lightly browned on each side. Repeat with the two remaining Dillas.

Cut each Dilla into four slices and serve.

linguine and chunky marinara sauce

There are some great marinara sauces in a jar, but it just makes you feel like a big fancy chef when you cook it yourself. And technically, if you use linguine, it's not spaghetti anymore so now you sound extra impressive. These little loopholes make this dish seem much more fancy than it really is. But no worries, it's still super budget friendly.

One 28-ounce can whole Roma tomatoes

One 8-ounce can tomato paste

2 garlic cloves, chopped

½ teaspoon sea salt

2 teaspoons Italian seasoning

1 cup water

½ cup diced red onions

½ cup diced green bell pepper

1 Roma tomato, diced

½ teaspoon pepper

1 cup rehydrated texture vegetable protein (TVP), optional

1 pound linguine, cooked according to package directions

Puree the tomatoes, tomato paste, and garlic in a blender.

Put into a medium stockpot over medium heat. Stir in water, salt, and Italian seasoning and bring to a boil.

Add the onions, bell pepper, and diced tomatoes. Reduce heat to low and simmer for 30 minutes. Serve over linguine.

MAKES 4 SERVINGS

QUICK AND EASY MEAL IDEA:
SPAGHETTI WHO?
(PAGE 45)

COOK'S TIP:

Unfortunately, every time I tried to make a smaller batch of this marinara sauce it just didn't turn out as good, so the recipe tends to make a considerable amount of extra sauce. But it freezes really well and can be used for Baked Ziti (page 123) or another batch of this Linguine with Chunky Marinara Sauce later.

filet o' tofish sandwiches

QUICK AND EASY
MEAL IDEA:
GIVE ME THAT FISH
(PAGE 46)

As an omnivore I never really liked fish, but as a vegan I love kelp. As it turns out, fish love kelp, too, which is where they get their "fishy" taste and smell. The base of this recipe can be used to make either Filet o' Tofish Sandwiches or Something's Fishy Tacos (page 165). There's enough batter in this recipe to make both, so save your leftover cornmeal batter in an airtight container in the refrigerator for up to 1 month and try those Something's Fishy Tacos, too.

If you're short on time, this recipe can always be fried instead of baked.

Canola oil spray

1 tablespoon plus 1 teaspoon kelp powder or granules

1 cup water

1 pound firm tofu, drained and cut into 4 slices lengthwise

½ cup coarse yellow cornmeal

1 cup panko bread crumbs

1 teaspoon garlic powder

1 teaspoon paprika

1 tablespoon nutritional yeast

¼ teaspoon sea salt

4 hamburger buns

1 recipe Tartar Sauce (page 202)

4 slices vegan cheddar or American cheese

Preheat the oven to 400° F. Lightly oil a baking sheet.

Whisk water with 1 teaspoon kelp powder in a shallow dish. Add the tofu and marinate for at least 10 minutes.

In another shallow dish mix the cornmeal, panko, 1 tablespoon kelp powder, garlic powder, paprika, nutritional yeast, and salt.

Dredge the tofu in the cornmeal mixture, completely covering both sides, and place on the cookie sheet. Repeat until all four slices are covered. Mist the top of each filet with oil. Bake for 40 minutes.

Assemble sandwiches by spreading Tartar Sauce evenly among buns. Layer half of the buns with vegan cheddar, top with filet, then top with the remaining half of the hamburger bun.

fool-your-friends tacos

MAKES 12 TACOS

QUICK AND EASY
MEAL IDEA:

BAJA CALIFORNIA DINNER
(PAGE 44)

COOK'S TIP:

You can play around with the color of bell pepper you choose to use. I prefer red and yellow, but green, purple, and orange also work well.

In my opinion, Mexican food is an awesome way to fool your meat-eating friends into eating vegan. And if you're a meat eater yourself, somewhere between sucking the taco sauce off your fingers and licking the plate after your fourth taco, you'll think to yourself, those were some darn good tacos, and you won't even have missed the meat. Trust me.

Just a note: I like to just enjoy what I call "the essence" of the taco and top only with tomatoes and taco sauce. If you like other toppings, feel free to pile them on!

1 cup vegetable stock
1½ teaspoons hickory liquid smoke
1 cup textured vegetable protein (TVP)
1 tablespoon canola oil
½ cup diced red onion
½ cup diced red bell pepper
½ cup diced yellow bell pepper
1 tablespoons water
2 tablespoons Taco Seasoning Mix (page 201)
12 taco shells or corn tortillas
½ medium tomato, chopped
Taco sauce of your choice

Bring the stock and liquid smoke to a boil in a small pot. Remove it from the heat, add the TVP, and let sit for 5 minutes.

Warm the oil in a medium saucepan over medium-high heat. Add the onion and sauté for 1 minute. Add red and yellow bell peppers and sauté for an additional minute.

Add the rehydrated TVP, Taco Seasoning Mix, and water. Cook until all the water has been absorbed and Taco Seasoning Mix has been evenly distributed.

Lightly toast the taco shells or soften the corn tortillas in a microwave for 30 seconds. Fill with the TVP mixture and then top with tomatoes and taco sauce.

fresh mex burritos

These burritos are incredibly versatile—if you want a little kick add the green chilies, and if you happen to have some vegan cheese lying around, feel free to throw it in. The burritos are great with or without vegan cheese, so don't run out to the store if you don't have it on hand.

One 15-ounce can pinto beans, drained and rinsed

1 cup frozen corn

2 tablespoon green chilies, optional

¼ cup vegetable stock

Four 8- or 12-inch tortillas

½ cup chopped fresh cilantro, loosely packed and chopped

1 medium tomato, diced

1 green onion, chopped

4 leaves green lettuce or romaine

Juice of 1 lime

1 avocado, cut into strips

¼ cup shredded vegan cheddar, optional

¼ cup shredded vegan mozzarella, optional

Vegan sour cream

Chunky Fresh Salsa Picada (page 194) or Pico de Gallo (page 199)

Simmer the beans, corn, and green chilies (if using) in vegetable stock until the stock is absorbed.

Lay out the tortillas and evenly distribute the beans and remaining ingredients among the tortillas. Roll and serve with sour cream and salsa.

MAKES 4 BURRITOS

QUICK AND EASY
MEAL IDEA:
CALIFORNIA FRESH MEX
(PAGE 41)

chik'n seitan

MAKES 1 POUND SEITAN

**QUICK AND EASY
MEAL IDEAS:**
SOUTHERN NIGHTS
(PAGE 44),
SOUTHERN FRIED SPECIAL
(PAGE 45), AND ALICIA'S
CHIK'N AND WAFFLES
(PAGE 46)

I don't know how my life was complete before I discovered the wonders of seitan. It has a chickenlike texture and the versatility to be marinated, battered, fried, baked, grilled, or pan-seared and added to any recipe that traditionally uses chicken. This recipe makes one pound, which usually serves four people. However, this recipe can easily be doubled or tripled to accommodate a larger crowd.

SEITAN:
- ½ cup vital wheat gluten
- ¼ cup soy flour
- ½ cup water

BROTH:
- 2 ½ cups water
- ¼ cup nutritional yeast
- 2 tablespoons Bragg Liquid Aminos
- 1 teaspoon onion powder
- 1 heaping teaspoon dried sage
- ½ teaspoon dried thyme
- ¼ teaspoon dried oregano

To make the seitan:

Combine the wheat gluten and flour in a small bowl then stir in water until it forms a ball.

On a lightly floured surface knead the dough for a little less than a minute and flatten to ½ inch thick.

Cut into desired shape (strips, nuggets, "breast," etc.). Keep in mind that during the cooking process the seitan will double in size.

To make the broth:

Put all broth ingredients into a medium stockpot and bring to a boil. Add the seitan one piece at a time, being careful not to splash the hot broth.

Reduce heat, cover, and simmer for 40 to 50 minutes, or until the majority of the broth has evaporated. stirring every 10 minutes. Smaller cuts like nuggets require less time, so keep an eye on them.

fried chik'n seitan

Fried Chik'n Seitan isn't nearly as bad for you as traditional fried chicken, but it isn't exactly health food either. But damn it, it's delicious, and sometimes you just need delicious. Isn't that what comfort food is all about?

Canola or peanut oil

½ cup soy milk

1 cup unbleached all-purpose flour

1 teaspoon sea salt

1 tablespoon paprika

½ teaspoon garlic powder

¼ teaspoon freshly ground black pepper

1 recipe Chik'n Seitan (page 138), cut into whatever shape you desire

Heat the oil in a large frying pan or deep-fryer to 375° F.

Pour the soy milk into a small, shallow bowl and set aside.

Stir the flour, salt, paprika, garlic powder, and pepper together in a separate shallow dish and place next to the soy milk.

Dredge the seitan in the flour mixture, then the soy milk, then the flour again, and place it in the hot oil.

Fry until golden brown on both sides. Remove from the oil and drain on paper towels.

QUICK AND EASY
MEAL IDEA:
SOUTHERN NIGHTS
(PAGE 44)

oven-fried chik'n seitan

MAKES 4 SERVINGS

**QUICK AND EASY
MEAL IDEA:**

ALICIA'S CHIK'N AND
WAFFLES (PAGE 46)

Fried Chik'n Seitan is one of the hallmarks of vegan comfort food, but if you simply cannot bear to fry it and want a healthier option, I highly recommend this Oven-fried Chik'n Seitan. It has all the goodness of the fried version without all that extra fat.

Canola oil spray

¾ cup soy milk or oat milk

½ teaspoon whole-grain mustard

1 cup panko bread crumbs

¼ teaspoon pepper

1 teaspoon dried thyme

2 teaspoon paprika

½ teaspoon cayenne pepper

½ teaspoon garlic powder

1 recipe Chik'n Seitan (page 138), cut into desired shape

Preheat the oven to 375° F. Oil a cookie sheet or line it with nonstick foil.

Whisk the soy milk with the mustard and set aside.

Combine the panko, pepper, thyme, paprika, cayenne, and garlic powder in a shallow dish and set next to the soy milk.

Dredge the seitan in soy milk and then the panko mixture.

Place the seitan on the oiled cookie sheet. Mist the top of the seitan with canola oil.

Bake for 40 to 45 minutes (30 to 35 minutes if using nugget-sized seitan), until golden brown.

Spicy oven-fried chik'n Seitan

There are three distinct types of traditional Southern soul food: syrupy-sweet, burn-your-mouth spicy, and straight-to-your-thighs fatty. This Spicy Oven-fried Chik'n Seitan fills the bill on the burn-your-mouth spicy without the straight-to-your-thighs fatty, and if you're still craving something that's a little syrupy-sweet, just pour yourself a glass of Southern sweet tea and you'll be set to go.

MAKES 4 SERVINGS

Quick and Easy Meal Idea:
Southern Fried Special (page 45)

Canola oil spray

¾ cup soy milk or oat milk

2 tablespoons hot sauce

1 cup panko bread crumbs

¼ teaspoon pepper

1 teaspoon dried thyme

2 teaspoons paprika

1½ teaspoon cayenne pepper

½ teaspoon garlic powder

1 teaspoon red pepper flakes

1 recipe Chik'n Seitan (page 138), cut into desired shape

> ## Cook's Tip:
>
> Everyone has a different interpretation of spicy, so the spices are set at about a medium in this recipe. Feel free to up the cayenne, red pepper flakes, or hot sauce if you require a bit more heat.

Preheat the oven to 375° F. Oil a cookie sheet or cover it with nonstick foil.

Whisk the soy milk with the hot sauce and set aside.

In a shallow dish, combine the panko, pepper, thyme, paprika, cayenne, garlic powder, and red pepper flakes, and set next to the soy milk.

Dredge the seitan in the soy milk mixture and then panko, until each piece of seitan is completely coated with panko mixture.

Place the seitan on the oiled cookie sheet. Mist the top of the seitan with canola oil.

Bake for 40 to 45 minutes (30 to 35 minutes if using nugget-sized seitan), until golden brown.

pecan-crusted seitan cutlets

MAKES 4 SERVINGS

QUICK AND EASY
MEAL IDEA:
PUMPKIN PECAN
PERFECTION (PAGE 47)

I have an unusual obsession with pecans. For me they are like the candy of the nut world. They are buttery, slightly sweet, and great chopped up, sprinkled over salads, in muffins, and on cereal. They are also incredibly good ground up and tossed with corn flakes to make these Pecan-crusted Seitan Cutlets.

Canola oil

2 cups corn flakes

½ cup pecans

1 teaspoon sugar

½ teaspoon onion powder

½ cup oat milk

1 tablespoon powdered egg replacer

1 recipe Chik'n Seitan (page 138), cut into large strips or mini chik'n breasts

Preheat the oven to 400° F. Liberally oil a cookie sheet.

Put the corn flakes, pecans, sugar, and onion powder in a food processor and grind until the mixture becomes a coarse powder. Transfer to a small shallow bowl.

In another small bowl, whisk the oat milk with the powdered egg replacer.

Dip the seitan pieces into the milk mixture, then into corn flake mixture, and place on the well-oiled cookie sheet. Repeat until each piece is completely coated. Drizzle or spray a light mist of canola oil over the seitan pieces.

Bake for 25 minutes.

spicy buffalo bites

Spicy Buffalo Bites are the vegan answer to buffalo wings. The key is to fry them until they are golden and crispy and toss them in the buffalo sauce just before serving, to preserve their crisp outer layers. You can eat them on their own or with a side of carrots, celery, and Blue Cheeze Dressing (page 185).

MAKES 4 SERVINGS

QUICK AND EASY
MEAL IDEA:
GAME DAY (PAGE 46)

  Canola or peanut oil

  ½ cup unbleached all-purpose flour

  ½ cup whole wheat flour

  1 teaspoon paprika

  1 teaspoon cayenne pepper

  ¼ teaspoon freshly ground black pepper

  1 cup plain soy milk

  1 recipe Chik'n Seitan (page 138), cut into 1-inch bites or nuggets

SAUCE:

  ½ cup hot sauce

  1 tablespoon maple syrup

  1 tablespoon vegan Worcestershire sauce

Heat the oil in a large frying pan or deep fryer to 375° F.

In a shallow dish, combine the all-purpose flour, whole wheat flour, paprika, cayenne, and black pepper.

Pour the soy milk into a separate shallow dish.

Dredge the seitan in the flour mixture, then soy milk, and then back in the flour. Fry until a deep brown on both sides. Remove from the oil and place on a plate covered with paper towels to catch any extra oil while the bites cool.

To make the sauce:

Mix together hot sauce, maple syrup, and Worcestershire sauce.

To serve the Spicy Buffalo Bites:

Add the seitan bites to a large bowl, pour in the sauce, and toss until all of the bites are covered.

Sloppy Josephs

MAKES 4 SERVINGS

QUICK AND EASY
MEAL IDEAS:
SLOPPY JALOPY
(PAGE 43)

Until very recently the only sloppy joe I knew came in a can and all you had to do was add a little TVP to have a great sandwich. For me sloppy joes are the ultimate in comfort food. They are sweet, smoky, and drip all over your hands and plate. Real comfort food requires at least four double-ply napkins to make it through the meal. These Sloppy Josephs deliver on all the requirements without any high fructose corn syrup and preservatives like the canned stuff.

1 cup vegetable stock

1 tablespoon hickory liquid smoke

1 cup textured vegetable protein (TVP)

1 cup tomato sauce

¼ cup ketchup

¼ cup BBQ Sauce (page 191)

1 tablespoon light brown sugar

¼ teaspoon dry mustard

2 tablespoons vegan Worchestershire sauce

1 tablespoon white vinegar

1 tablespoon canola oil

¼ cup diced white or yellow onion

¼ cup chopped green bell pepper

8 whole wheat or spelt hamburger buns, lightly toasted

In a small saucepan, heat the stock and liquid smoke almost to boiling. Add the TVP to the stock and set aside.

Whisk the tomato sauce, ketchup, BBQ Sauce, brown sugar, dry mustard, Worchestershire sauce, and vinegar in a medium saucepan over medium heat. Lower the heat, cover, and simmer for 15 minutes, stirring occasionally.

Warm the oil over medium heat in a large skillet. Add the onion and bell pepper and sauté for 3 minutes. Add rehydrated TVP and continue to cook for 2 minutes.

Add the tomato sauce mixture to the TVP and onion mixture and stir until completely combined.

Spoon Sloppy Josephs mixture onto toasted hamburger buns and serve.

homemade veggie burger

MAKES 4 BURGERS

QUICK AND EASY
MEAL IDEA:
THE HAMBURGER HALL
OF FAME (PAGE 47)

I made this veggie burger just to prove to myself I could do it. It made me feel very accomplished. Go ahead, try it for yourself. You'll feel accomplished, too.

¾ cup vegetable stock

1 tablespoon hickory liquid smoke

1 cup textured vegetable protein (TVP)

1 tablespoon vegan Worcestershire sauce

¼ cup diced red onions

¼ cup diced green bell peppers

1 garlic clove, chopped

¼ cup diced cremini or shiitake mushrooms, stems removed

2 tablespoons ketchup

2 tablespoons vital wheat gluten

¼ teaspoon sea salt

⅛ teaspoon pepper

2 tablespoons canola oil

4 whole wheat or spelt hamburger buns

OPTIONAL TOPPINGS:

Vegan mayonnaise

Mustard

Ketchup

Sweet relish

4 slices tomato

4 thin slices red onion

4 leaves green leaf or romaine lettuce

Bring the stock and liquid smoke to a boil in a small pot. Add the TVP and let sit for 5 minutes.

Put the rehydrated TVP, Worcestershire sauce, onion, bell pepper, garlic, and mushroom in a food processor and pulse until vegetables are minced and incorporated into the TVP.

Empty the TVP mixture into a large bowl and add the ketchup, salt, pepper, and finally the wheat gluten—this should be done with your hands, if possible.

Form into four patties, about ¼ inch thick. Refrigerate the patties, covered, for 30 minutes to an hour; they can also be refrigerated overnight.

Warm the oil in a large skillet over medium heat. Cook the veggie burger patties until they are brown on both sides. Place on a bun, add toppings of your choice, and enjoy.

kale with grits cakes

MAKES 4 SERVINGS

QUICK AND EASY
MEAL IDEA:
SOPHISTICATED SOUL
(PAGE 45)

I am fortunate to have several local farms nearby and a co-op that supports them. I like to use a mix of different types of young kale. If you don't happen to have your choice of kale, just choose whichever is available at your local grocer. You really can't go wrong.

GRITS CAKES:

2 cups water

1 cup instant white grits

½ cup shredded vegan Monterey Jack cheese

½ teaspoon cayenne pepper

KALE:

5 garlic cloves, minced

½ cup sliced white onions

1 tablespoon extra virgin olive oil

2 large bunches kale, torn

4 cups vegetable stock

½ teaspoon pepper

Lightly oil an 8×8-inch baking dish.

To make the grits:

Bring water to a boil in a medium saucepan. Whisk in the grits and cook for 5 minutes, stirring frequently. Add the Monterey Jack and cayenne and stir to combine.

Pour the grits into the baking dish and cool at room temperature. When the grits are cool, cut into four cakes, whatever shape you would like. For crispier cakes bake for 10 minutes at 350° F.

To make the kale:

Sauté the garlic and onion in olive oil in a medium saucepan for 1 minute. Add the kale and stock and bring to a boil. Sprinkle with pepper and stir. Reduce heat, cover, and simmer for 45 minutes. Drain off the liquid.

Position cakes in the center of your serving plate and top with drained kale.

red beans with quinoa

Red beans and rice, watch out! There's a new sheriff in town and its name is quinoa. Quinoa plays an exceptional accompanying role to the red beans in this dish, soaking up all the flavors of the sauce, giving you a little taste of red bean heaven in every bite.

MAKES 4 SERVINGS

QUICK AND EASY
MEAL IDEA:
THE MEAN BEAN
(PAGE 42)

½ cup diced yellow onion

½ cup diced green bell pepper

1 tablespoon canola oil

2 garlic cloves, minced

Two 14-ounce cans red kidney beans

½ cup BBQ Sauce (page 191)

1½ teaspoon hot sauce

1 tablespoon vegan Worcestershire sauce

½ teaspoon pepper

2 cups cooked quinoa, hot

Sauté the onion and bell pepper in canola oil in a medium saucepan for 2 minutes. Add the garlic and cook for an additional minute. Add the kidney beans, BBQ Sauce, hot sauce, Worchestershire sauce, and pepper. Cook, stirring frequently, until completely warmed through.

Divide the warm quinoa evenly among four serving plates and top with kidney beans.

lemon and caper linguine

MAKES 4 SERVINGS

QUICK AND EASY
MEAL IDEA:
ITALIAN SIMPLICITY
(PAGE 46)

This dish is light, quick, and perfect when you're short on time. You can steam the broccoli separately or, to save on time and dishes, toss in the raw broccoli during the last two minutes of boiling the linguine.

3 tablespoons extra virgin olive oil

3 garlic cloves, crushed and minced

2½ tablespoons capers

¼ cup fresh lemon juice

2 cups broccoli florets, steamed

½ pound linguine, cooked according to package directions

Warm 1 tablespoon of olive oil in a medium saucepan over medium heat. Add the garlic and sauté just until it becomes fragrant, about 30 seconds. Add capers and sauté an additional 30 seconds.

Remove from the heat and add lemon juice, broccoli, linguine, and the remaining 2 tablespoons of olive oil. Toss until thoroughly combined. Serve warm.

"pepperoni" mini pizzas

Feel free to substitute crumbled vegan breakfast sausage or vegetables and fruit (broccoli, spinach, pineapple, bell pepper) for pepperoni. Get creative! Once you have the basic ingredients on hand you can go wild with the combinations.

MAKES 6 MINI PIZZAS

QUICK AND EASY
MEAL IDEA:
MOBILE PIZZERIA
(PAGE 43)

3 English muffins

⅓ cup Pizza Sauce (page 190)

¾ cup shredded vegan meltable mozzarella

1 package sliced vegetarian pepperoni

Preheat the oven to 400° F. (or 350° F if you are using a toaster oven).

Split the English muffins in half. Spread 1 tablespoon of Pizza Sauce on each half.

Sprinkle cheese on the muffins, about 2 tablespoons per pizza. Arrange four or five pepperoni slices on each muffin half.

Bake until the cheese melts, about 15 minutes in a conventional oven or 12 minutes in a toaster oven.

portobello fajitas

QUICK AND EASY
MEAL IDEA:
THE MIGHTY MUSHROOM
(PAGE 43)

I've never met a plant-based food that I wouldn't at least try to eat, although I have to admit that mushrooms have tested this claim since I was a child. Over the last seven years I've begun to make some headway in my quest to like them, and these fajitas are a big help! I like mushrooms heavily marinated in balsamic vinegar, but if you want the pure taste of portobellos, feel free to take down the balsamic vinegar to ¼ or ½ cup.

3 large portobello mushrooms, stems removed and cut into strips

¾ cup balsamic vinegar

4 tablespoons canola oil

½ large red onion, cut into wedges

1 medium bell pepper, sliced thin

1 teaspoon chili powder

1 teaspoon ground cumin

1 teaspoon ground coriander

4 large flour tortillas

1 large tomato, chopped

½ cup fresh cilantro, chopped

Vegan sour cream

Chunky Fresh Salsa Picada (page 194) or Pico de Gallo (page 199)

Marinate the mushrooms in balsamic vinegar for about 20 minutes. Remove the mushrooms from the marinade and set aside.

Heat 2 tablespoons of the oil in a large saucepan or frying pan over medium heat. Cook the mushrooms for about 3 minutes, turning often. Add the remaining 2 tablespoons of oil, the bell peppers, onions, chili powder, cumin, and coriander. Cook for an additional 5 minutes, stirring often.

Heat the tortillas for 15 seconds in the microwave to soften, and evenly distribute the mushroom mixture in each tortilla. Top with the tomatoes, cilantro, sour cream, and salsa.

Spicy Soba noodles in peanut Sauce

Soba noodles are Japanese spaghetti-style noodles traditionally made of buckwheat flour. This is a hearty stir-fry dish with a hint of sweetness and just the right amount of heat from the red pepper flakes. You don't need much more than a light soup to make this a complete meal.

One 8-ounce package soba noodles

4 medium carrots, peeled and julienne cut

1 cup broccoli florets, chopped

1 cup frozen peas

1 tablespoon peanut oil

½ large red bell pepper, cut into thin strips

3 green onions, white part and ½ inch green part, chopped

½ cup diced celery

½ cup Thai Peanut Sauce (page 204) or prepared peanut sauce

1 tablespoon maple syrup, optional

1 teaspoon red pepper flakes

Freshly ground black pepper to taste

Prepare the noodles per the instructions on the package, minus 1 minute. Drain, do not rinse, and set aside.

While the soba is cooking, steam the carrots, broccoli, and peas until the carrots are tender, about 5 minutes.

Warm the oil over medium-high heat in a large saucepan or wok. Add the bell pepper, green onion, and celery. Sauté for 2 minutes. Add the steamed vegetables and cook for an additional 3 or 4 minutes. Add the soba noodles and mix thoroughly. Slowly stir in the peanut sauce and maple syrup, if using, until noodles and vegetables are thoroughly coated. Sprinkle with red pepper flakes and season with pepper to taste. Serve warm.

MAKES 4 SERVINGS

QUICK AND EASY
MEAL IDEA:
SOBA SIESTA (PAGE 42)

spinach lasagna

MAKES 6 TO 8 SERVINGS

QUICK AND EASY
MEAL IDEA:
A LASAGNA YOU CAN'T
REFUSE (PAGE 47)

When most people think of lasagna they think of layers and layers of noodles topped with marinara sauce and tons of ooey-gooey cheese. As I played around with the next two recipes, I quickly discovered that both of them stand up just fine on their own without any type of vegan cheese. I've left both options open here: you can use either meltable vegan mozzarella, for a more traditional lasagna, or nutritional yeast.

Canola oil for the pan

Three 10-ounce packages frozen spinach, steamed and water pressed out

½ teaspoon pepper

3 garlic cloves, minced

½ block firm tofu, drained, pressed, and mashed

1 teaspoon Italian seasoning

¼ teaspoon nutritional yeast

⅛ teaspoon sea salt

4 cups store-bought marinara sauce

9 to 12 uncooked lasagna noodles

2 cups shredded meltable vegan mozzarella or ½ cup nutritional yeast

Preheat the oven to 350°F. Coat a 12×8×2-inch (about 3 quarts) baking dish with canola oil.

Combine the spinach, pepper, and garlic in a large bowl.

In a separate small bowl, stir together the tofu, Italian seasoning, nutritional yeast, and salt.

Pour 1 cup of marinara sauce over the bottom of the baking dish and cover with a layer of uncooked lasagna noodles. Spread half of the spinach and half of the tofu mixture evenly over the first layer of noodles, cover with 1 cup of marinara sauce, and sprinkle on 2 tablespoons of nutritional yeast or ½ cup mozzarella, then repeat (marinara, noodles, spinach, tofu, nutritional yeast or mozzarella).

Place one more layer of noodles on top, for a total of three noodle layers, pour in the remaining marinara sauce, and sprinkle with the remaining nutritional yeast or mozzarella.

Pour ⅓ cup water around the edge of the baking dish and cover with aluminum foil.

Bake for 1 hour. Let stand to cool for at least 10 minutes and serve warm.

vegetable lasagna

MAKES 6 TO 8 SERVINGS

QUICK AND EASY
MEAL IDEA:

ITALIANO CLASSICO
(PAGE 46)

Let's say you're not exactly in the mood for Spinach Lasagna. No worries, just add more vegetables! The key to this recipe is preparation. If all the ingredients are sliced and diced in advance, it will save you a lot of time. I recommend buying shredded carrots and using a food processor fitted with a slice blade to cut the zucchini and yellow squash.

Canola oil for the pan

1 cup shredded carrots

1 medium zucchini, sliced thin

½ medium yellow squash, sliced thin

One 10-ounce package frozen spinach, steamed and water pressed out

½ block firm tofu, drained, pressed, and mashed

1 teaspoon Italian seasoning

1 teaspoon nutritional yeast

⅛ teaspoon sea salt plus more, to taste

2 cups shredded meltable vegan mozzarella or ½ cup nutritional yeast

4 cups store-bought marinara sauce

9 to 12 uncooked lasagna noodles

Freshly ground pepper to taste

Preheat the oven to 350° F.

Coat a 12×8×2 inch (about 3 quarts) baking dish with canola oil.

Put the carrots, zucchini, squash, spinach, salt, and pepper in a large bowl and stir until combined.

Combine the tofu, Italian seasoning, nutritional yeast, and ⅛ teaspoon salt in a separate bowl. Set aside.

Pour 1 cup marinara sauce over the bottom of the baking dish and place a layer of lasagna noodles over it.

Spread half of the vegetable mixture and half of the tofu mixture evenly over the first layer of noodles, cover with 1 cup marinara sauce and sprinkle with 2 tablespoons of nutritional yeast or ½ cup of mozzarella, then repeat (marinara, noodles, vegetables, tofu, nutritional yeast or mozzarella).

Place one more layer of noodles on top, for a total of three noodle layers, pour in the remaining marinara sauce, and sprinkle with the last tablespoon of nutritional yeast or remaining mozzarella. Pour ⅓ cup water around the edge of the baking dish and cover with aluminum foil.

Bake for 1 hour. Let stand to cool for at least 10 minutes and serve warm.

Super chicks

MAKES 4 SANDWICHES

QUICK AND EASY
MEAL IDEAS:
FAT CHANCE (PAGE 42),
TOO HOT TO HANDLE
(PAGE 43). AND A THOU-
SAND MILES FROM HOME
(PAGE 47)

Faux-chicken patties and chicken nuggets are the reason I went vegetarian. This might sound backward, but there is not an animal on this planet that can duplicate the great taste of faux-chicken patties. But sometimes even a devoted fan such as myself likes to change it up a bit. Here are three great ways to add a little twist to the norm.

You can also substitute Fried Chik'n Seitan (page 139) for the store-bought breaded chik'n patties.

THE HOT CHICK

    4 breaded faux-chicken patties
    1 cup hot sauce
    ⅓ cup vegan mayonnaise
    2 tablespoons vegan bacon bits
    4 whole wheat or spelt hamburger buns
    4 leaves romaine, red leaf, green leaf, or Bibb lettuce
    1 medium Roma tomato, sliced thin

Preheat the oven to 425° F.

Marinate patties in hot sauce for 10 minutes. Remove the patties from the hot sauce and place them on a baking sheet lined with foil. Bake for 15 minutes, turning them halfway through.

While the patties are baking, stir together the mayonnaise and bacon bits. Toast the hamburger buns. To assemble, spread the mayonnaise mixture on both sides of each hamburger bun. Put the patties, lettuce, and tomato on the sandwiches and close them up.

The Fat Chick (Healthy Fats, of Course)

4 breaded faux-chicken patties

4 whole wheat or spelt hamburger buns

1 recipe Guacamole (page 195)

Alfalfa, clover, or broccoli sprouts

4 slices vegan mozzarella

Preheat the oven to 425° F.

Bake patties for 15 minutes, turning halfway through (if using Fried Chik'n Seitan, skip this step).

Toast the hamburger buns. Divide patties, guacamole, sprouts, and cheese among the 4 buns and enjoy.

1000 Chicks

4 breaded faux-chicken patties

4 whole wheat or spelt hamburger buns

1 recipe Thousand Island Dressing (page 186)

4 leaves romaine, red leaf, green leaf, or Bibb lettuce

¼ cup diced white onions

4 slices vegan cheddar

Preheat the oven to 425° F.

Bake patties for 15 minutes, turning halfway through (if using Fried Chik'n Seitan, skip this step).

Toast the hamburger buns. Spread Thousand Island Dressing on the hamburger buns. Divide the patties lettuce, onions, and cheese among hamburger buns and enjoy.

triple b's

QUICK AND EASY
MEAL IDEAS:
BACKYARD BBQ
(PAGE 45), THE STEAK
DINNER (PAGE 45), AND
EAST MEETS WEST
(PAGE 47)

Ah yes, Triple Burgers! I've had more than my fair share of veggie burgers, and the plain lettuce, tomato, pickles, and mayo combo gets old quick. Here are three great ways to jazz up a veggie burger. For all of these I use a nonstick indoor grill, but an outdoor grill will work just as well. To ensure that the burgers don't stick to the outdoor grill, cook burgers on foil with a little oil.

BBQ Burger

    4 store-bought veggie burger patties
    ¾ cup BBQ Sauce (page 191)
    4 whole wheat or spelt hamburger buns
    4 leaves romaine or green leaf lettuce
    4 slices vegan cheddar or American cheese
    ½ small red onion, sliced thin
    1 tablespoon plus 1 teaspoon sweet relish

Heat the grill to medium. Baste both sides of the veggie burgers with BBQ Sauce and grill for 20 minutes, turning every 5 minutes and basting with more sauce at each turn.

Add the remaining BBQ Sauce to each side of the buns and build burgers as you like with the above ingredients, using 1 teaspoon of relish for each burger.

Teriyaki Burger

½ cup Teriyaki Sauce (page 203)

1 tablespoon plus 1 teaspoon light brown sugar, optional

4 store-bought veggie burger patties

4 slices fresh pineapple cut into ½-inch-thick rings

4 whole wheat or spelt hamburger buns

Whisk the Teriyaki Sauce with brown sugar, if using. Heat the grill to medium. Baste both sides of the veggie burger with Teriyaki Sauce and grill for 20 minutes, turning every 5 minutes and basting with more sauce at each turn.

While the burgers are cooking on the grill also grill the pineapples, turning every 5 minutes as well.

Toast the hamburger buns and build the burgers with the above ingredients as you like.

A-1 Burger

4 store-bought veggie burger patties

½ cup steak sauce

½ small Spanish or white onion, sliced thin

½ small red bell pepper, sliced thin

4 whole wheat or spelt hamburger buns

1 Roma tomato, sliced thin

Heat the grill to medium. Baste both sides of the veggie burger with steak sauce and grill for 20 minutes, turning every 5 minutes and basting with more sauce at each turn.

During the last 5 minutes of grilling, place the onion and red bell pepper on the grill.

Toast the hamburger buns and assemble as you like with the above ingredients.

Sun-dried tomato and roasted red pepper panini

MAKES 2 PANINI

QUICK AND EASY
MEAL IDEA:
TOUR OF ITALY
(PAGE 43)

I woke up one Saturday morning wanting some panini, but, alas, I had no panini press. So I went to all the foo-foo cooking stores and discovered that panini presses cost nearly $100. However, this story has a happy ending because, as it turns out, any old electric grill will do when making panini. I like using one that is endorsed by a popular ex-boxer (hint, hint). And fresh bread makes all the difference so, if you can, get it fresh from a local bakery or local grocer.

4 slices sourdough bread

Vegan mayonnaise

8 slices meltable vegan mozzarella

1 roasted red pepper, sliced thin

4 oil-packed sun-dried tomatoes, sliced thin

½ small shallot, sliced thin

½ cup sunflower seed sprouts

8 basil leaves

Spread just enough mayo on each slice of bread to thinly coat it. Then layer each slice of bread with two slices of cheese.

Evenly distribute the peppers, tomatoes, shallots, sunflower sprouts, and basil between two slices of bread.

Put the sandwiches together and grill until the cheese is completely melted, about 5 minutes.

Simple croissant sandwiches

MAKES 6 SANDWICHES

When I was in middle school and high school there was nothing I loved more than walking to the local grocery store on a summer day and getting a vegetarian croissant sandwich from the deli. Thanks to these great premade rolls, all I have to do is roll and bake and I can enjoy them again in a cruelty-free way. There aren't too many constraints around this recipe. I give you the ingredients and you choose the portions you want to go on each sandwich. It's teamwork!

Quick and Easy Meal Idea: Deli at Your Desk (page 44)

6 Pillsbury Big and Flaky Crescent Rolls,
    prepared according to package directions

Vegan mayonnaise

Stone-ground mustard

1 small tomato, sliced thin

½ small red onion, sliced thin

1 avocado, pitted and cut into thin strips

2 romaine lettuce leaves, hard stalk removed from
    center and cut into 6 pieces

Alfalfa, clover, or broccoli sprouts

Cut the rolls in half as evenly as possible. Spread vegan mayonnaise and mustard on each slice and layer with toppings as you desire.

Note: Traditionally Pillsbury Big and Flaky Crescent Rolls have been considered vegan. However, they do contain Diacetyl Acid Tartaric Ester of Monoglyceride (DATEM), which is an emulsifier that binds to gluten. DATEM comes from both plant and animal sources; however, Pillsbury has not stated officially which source they use.

tacos pecadillo

MAKES 12 TACOS

QUICK AND EASY
MEAL IDEA:
THE LITTLE SIN
(PAGE 47)

In Spanish, pecadillo *means "little sin," and these tacos truly live up to their name! This is not your average taco; it has a pleasant, unique flavor, and a kick that only jalapeños can give. A warning: the longer the jalapeños sit, the hotter the tacos become. If you really like your tacos hot, make this the night before and let that jalapeño do its work!*

1 cup vegetable stock
1 tablespoon hickory liquid smoke
1 heaping cup textured vegetable protein (TVP)
2 tablespoons canola oil
½ cup chopped red onion
2 garlic cloves, minced
1 tablespoon chili powder
1 teaspoon ground cumin
1 teaspoon paprika
One 14.5-ounce can diced tomatoes, with juices
1 medium jalapeño pepper, minced
12 taco shells or 12 corn tortillas
2 ripe medium tomatoes, chopped
¼ head romaine lettuce, chopped
1 recipe Guacamole (page 195)

Heat the stock and liquid smoke almost to boiling. Remove from the heat, add the TVP to the stock, and set aside. Heat the oil in a medium skillet over medium heat. Add the onion and sauté for 3 minutes. Add the garlic and sauté for another minute.

Add the rehydrated TVP, chili powder, cumin, and paprika, and cook until TVP absorbs the spices, about 5 minutes, stirring occasionally.

Increase the heat to medium-high and add the tomatoes, their juices, and the jalapeño. Allow to boil and thicken, about 2 minutes. Remove from the heat.

Lightly toast the taco shells for 1 minute, or soften the corn tortillas in the microwave for 30 seconds.

Fill each taco shell with the TVP mixture, fresh tomatoes, lettuce, and Guacamole.

something's fishy tacos

The first time I heard of fish tacos I was drifting through the streets of Tijuana with my mother, grandmother, and little brother, going from vendor to vendor. I was never one to eat fish so I passed them up, but isn't it funny that now that I'm a big old card-carrying vegan, I find myself making them all the time!

QUICK AND EASY
MEAL IDEA:
TOFU OF THE SEA
(PAGE 44)

½ cup plain soy milk, oat milk, or water

1 teaspoon kelp powder

1 pound firm or extra-firm tofu, drained and pressed

½ cup coarse cornmeal

1 cup panko bread crumbs

1 tablespoon kelp powder or granules

1 teaspoon garlic powder

1 teaspoon paprika

1 tablespoon nutritional yeast

¼ teaspoon salt

½ cup canola oil

Mango Salsa (page 196)

1 cup shredded green or red cabbage

10 corn tortillas

Lay tofu flat on its widest side and cut in ¼-inch slices (9–10 slices). In a shallow dish whisk together soy/oat milk or water and kelp powder; set aside.

Stir together cornmeal, panko, kelp powder, garlic, paprika, nutritional yeast, and salt in another shallow dish until combined.

Heat canola oil over medium-high heat.

Dredge tofu slices through the soy milk mixture, then through the cornmeal mixture until completely covering all sides and fry in canola oil until brown on both sides. Remove from oil and allow tofu to rest on a plate or serving dish covered with paper towels to absorb the oil. Repeat until all tofu slices have been fried.

To assemble, place 1 piece of Tofish on each tortilla and divide shredded cabbage and mango salsa among tacos.

penny-pinching tacos

MAKES 12 TACOS

QUICK AND EASY
MEAL IDEA:
TIJUANA TORPEDO
(PAGE 45)

Corn tortillas are a fabulously frugal food. They come in packages of at least twenty for under $3, and they freeze incredibly well. If you don't have the time or the resources to make homemade salsa, nine times out of ten your favorite Mexican restaurant will sell their salsa fairly cheaply, and it's way better than that store-bought stuff. It cuts down on my time in the kitchen and I still get fresh, wholesome ingredients.

One 15-ounce can vegetarian refried beans
12 soft corn tortillas
1 medium tomato, diced
1 cup shredded lettuce
Chunky Fresh Salsa Picada (page 194) or Pico de Gallo (page 199)

Warm the refried beans in a medium saucepan. Soften the tortillas in the microwave for 30 seconds.

Fill each tortilla with beans, tomatoes, and lettuce, and top with fresh salsa.

teriyaki rice bowl

My first exposure to Japanese food was at a little takeout place in Fresno, California. My favorite dish: crisp, fresh, lightly steamed veggies over rice with just a hint of teriyaki sauce, and vegetable tempura on the side. So simple, so delicious. I can't fly back to Fresno every time I have a craving, so this is my substitute. You can serve this dish as is or add a protein source like pan-fried strips of Chik'n Seitan (page 138) or fried tofu strips.

MAKES 2 RICE BOWLS

QUICK AND EASY
MEAL IDEA:
JAPANESE TAKEOUT
(PAGE 42)

1 cup jasmine rice

1 cup carrots, peeled and julienne cut

1 cup broccoli florets

1 cup sugar snap peas or green beans

3 green onions, chopped

½ cup Teriyaki Sauce (page 203)

Cook the rice according to the directions on the package.

Steam the carrots for 3 minutes. Add the broccoli and sugar snap peas and steam an additional 2 minutes.

Divide rice among the serving bowls and top with the steamed vegetables, green onions, and Teriyaki Sauce.

tuno tempeh sandwich

MAKES 4 SANDWICHES

QUICK AND EASY
MEAL IDEA:
A FISHY SITUATION
(PAGE 42)

I have never been a fan of fish. I don't know if it was my pet gold-fish "Speedy" or his predecessor, "Green Eggs and Ham," that made me disgusted at the idea of eating fish, but I just never warmed up to it. The only exception to this dislike was tuna; for some rea-son, the fact that it came in a can made it seem less fishy. I wish I had known then that I could make a cruelty-free tuna sandwich that tastes just as the original, if not better.

Tuno Tempeh also goes great on crackers.

One 8-ounce package tempeh, any variety
2 cups vegetable stock
¼ cup plus 2 tablespoons vegan mayonnaise
¼ cup plus 1 tablespoon sweet relish
¼ cup chopped red onion
½ teaspoon kelp powder
½ teaspoon stone-ground mustard
¼ cup diced celery
8 slices whole-grain or sprouted bread

Simmer the tempeh in stock for 25 minutes. Discard any excess stock and set the tempeh aside to cool.

Grate the cooled tempeh into a medium bowl. Add the may-onnaise, relish, onion, kelp powder, mustard, and celery, and stir to combine. Spoon onto the bread and close the sandwiches.

COOK'S TIP:

Feel free to add other healthy toppings to this sandwich, like sliced tomatoes or sprouts of your choice.

tuno melt

The first time I had a tuna melt was at a diner in Virginia at about two o'clock in the morning. From that moment on, it was my new late-night favorite, or so I thought. After going vegan and making my Tuno Tempeh Sandwich a couple of times, I decided to add a little vegan cheese and a slice of tomato to veganize my favorite diner dish. From the first bite of this new classic I was on cloud nine!

For a lower-fat version, skip the margarine and cook these sandwiches on a panini grill.

1 recipe Tuno Tempeh Sandwich (page 168)

4 slices meltable vegan mozzarella

4 thin slices tomato

4 tablespoons non-hydrogenated margarine

Assemble Tuna Tempeh Sandwiches according to directions. Add 1 slice of mozzarella and a tomato slice to each sandwich.

Melt 1 tablespoon of margarine in a large saucepan. Place 1 or 2 sandwiches in the margarine and cook until lightly browned on both sides. Repeat with the remaining sandwiches and serve warm.

MAKES 4 SANDWICHES

QUICK AND EASY
MEAL IDEA:
TUNO ME IS TO LOVE ME
(PAGE 42)

tuno casserole

QUICK AND EASY
MEAL IDEAS:
TUNI-ROLE SUPPER
(PAGE 47)

Casseroles are some of my favorite dishes because they require little effort, yet they are so filling. The mark of a truly good casserole is finding yourself on the couch 15 minutes after eating the casserole, rubbing your belly, with a huge grin on your face.

If you have been hesitant to experiment with oat milk, this recipe is a great one to try it in. It marries well with Cheezly mature white cheddar cheese, adding just the right taste and texture to the dish to have you on the couch, grinning and happy, in no time.

TUNO:

  1½ cups cooked garbanzo beans

  2 teaspoons dulse flakes

  ½ cup water

CASSEROLE:

  ¼ cup nonhydrogenated margarine

  ½ cup diced white onion

  ¼ cup unbleached all-purpose flour

  3½ cups plain oat milk or soy milk

  1¼ teaspoons sea salt

  ¼ teaspoon pepper

  1½ cups frozen peas

  2 cups Cheezly mature white cheddar, shredded

  One 12-ounce package penne pasta, cooked according
    to package directions

To make the Tuno:

Put the garbanzo beans, dulse flakes, and water into a small saucepan over medium-high heat. Cook until the mixture begins to boil, reduce heat, and simmer until all the water is absorbed.

To make the Tuno Casserole:

Preheat the oven to 400°F.

Melt the margarine in a medium stockpot over medium heat, add the onions, and cook until tender, about 2 to 3 minutes.

Stir the flour into the margarine and onion mixture. Add the oat milk, salt, and pepper. Cook, stirring frequently, until the sauce begins to thicken and bubble. Add the peas, chickpeas, 1 cup cheddar, and the pasta.

Mix thoroughly until sauce covers all the pasta. Sprinkle with the remaining 1 cup of cheddar and bake, uncovered, for 15 minutes.

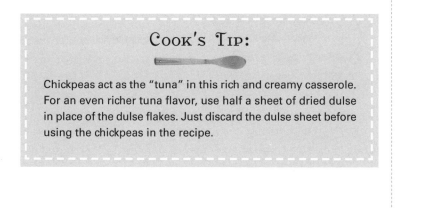

Cook's Tip:

Chickpeas act as the "tuna" in this rich and creamy casserole. For an even richer tuna flavor, use half a sheet of dried dulse in place of the dulse flakes. Just discard the dulse sheet before using the chickpeas in the recipe.

quick veggie casserole

QUICK AND EASY
MEAL IDEAS:
QUICK, FAST, AND IN A
HURRY (PAGE 47)

Like a lot of my recipes, this one came together in a moment of starvation and desperation. I was too tired to leave the house and too lazy to make a four-course meal. But there, shining in the cupboard, was that box of couscous, unopened since I'd bought it four months earlier. It all clicked. Enjoy!

Canola oil for the casserole dish
One 10-ounce package frozen mixed vegetables (carrots, corn, peas, and green beans)
½ cup couscous
¾ cup vegetable stock
½ cup chopped white onion
2 cups shredded vegan white cheddar or vegan meltable mozzarella
Sea salt to taste
Freshly ground pepper to taste

Preheat the oven to 350° F. Lightly oil a 2-quart casserole.

Boil vegetable stock in a medium sauce pan. Add couscous, reduce heat to a simmer, and cover. Cook until all the liquid has absorbed, about 5 minutes. Fluff with a fork.

Combine all the ingredients in a medium bowl, reserving ½ cup of cheese.

Spoon the couscous mixture into the casserole dish and sprinkle with the remaining ½ cup of cheese. Bake, uncovered, for 10 minutes.

veggie "meat" loaf

I think I might have been the only child in America who got excited by the words "We're having meatloaf for dinner." Something about meatloaf just makes you feel like you're right at home even if you're miles away.

1 tablespoon canola oil plus more for the pan

1¾ cups vegetable stock

4 teaspoons vegan Worcestershire sauce

3 teaspoons hickory liquid smoke

2 cups textured vegetable protein (TVP)

½ cup diced red onion

¼ cup diced red or green bell pepper

1 cup quick oats

1¾ cups ketchup

2 tablespoons vital wheat gluten

¼ teaspoon sea salt

¼ teaspoon pepper

¼ teaspoon garlic powder

MAKES 4 SERVINGS

QUICK AND EASY
MEAL IDEA:
MAMA'S HOME COOKING
(PAGE 44)

Preheat the oven to 375° F. Grease a loaf pan or baking sheet.

Bring the stock, 2 teaspoons Worcestershire sauce, and 2 teaspoons liquid smoke to a low boil in a small saucepan. Add the TVP, stir, and let sit for 5 minutes.

Warm 1 tablespoon canola oil in a small saucepan over medium heat. Add the onion and bell pepper and sauté for 2 minutes.

Put the onion mixture, rehydrated TVP, oats, 1¼ cup ketchup, wheat gluten, salt, black pepper, garlic powder, 2 teaspoons Worcestershire sauce, and 1 teaspoon liquid smoke in a large bowl. Stir until all the ingredients are combined. You can also use your hands to better mix all the ingredients.

Put the mixture into the prepared pan or shape it into a loaf and place it on a greased baking sheet. Bake for 40 minutes. Add the remaining ½ cup ketchup to the top of the loaf and bake for an additional 15 minutes.

Remove from the oven and let cool for 5 minutes. Serve warm.

veganized orange chik'n

MAKES 4 SERVINGS

QUICK AND EASY
MEAL IDEA:
CHINESE TAKE-IN
(PAGE 46)

There's this great little Chinese restaurant in my hometown that has a full vegan menu complete with Peking duck, sesame chicken, and my all-time favorite—orange chicken. This is my attempt at replicating their phenomenal recipe. You can substitute Chik'n Seitan (page 138) for tofu.

ORANGE SAUCE:

1 tablespoon minced fresh ginger

1 garlic clove, minced

1 tablespoon canola oil

½ teaspoon red pepper flakes

3 green onions, chopped

1 tablespoon mirin

3 tablespoons soy sauce or Bragg Liquid Aminos

3 tablespoons water

½ cup plus 2 tablespoons sugar

¼ cup plus 1 tablespoon white vinegar

¼ cup plus 1 tablespoon rice vinegar

¼ cup orange juice

2 tablespoons cornstarch or arrowroot

CHIK'N:

1 pound firm tofu

½ cup arrowroot or cornstarch (for the Fried Orange Chik'n)

Canola oil (for the Fried Orange Chik'n)

Canola oil spray (for the Baked Orange Chik'n)

To make the Orange Sauce:

Sauté the ginger and garlic in oil until fragrant, about 1 minute. Add the red pepper flakes, green onion, and mirin, and cook for an additional 1 minute.

Add the soy sauce, sugar, white vinegar, rice vinegar, and orange juice, and cook until boiling. Lower heat to a simmer and cook 5 minutes more.

174   QUICK AND EASY VEGAN COMFORT FOOD

Whisk in cornstarch and cook another 5 minutes or until the sauce begins to thicken. Then follow one of the following preparations.

Fried Veganized Orange Chik'n:

Freeze, thaw, drain, and press the tofu. Cut it into bite-size pieces.

Heat oil to 375° F in a deep fryer.

Put ½ cup cornstarch into a gallon-size plastic bag. Add the tofu and shake until it is completely coated. Fry in small batches until golden brown on all sides. Watch carefully, as they can burn quickly.

Add the fried tofu to the Orange Sauce and coat every piece. Serve warm.

Baked Veganized Orange Chik'n:

Preheat the oven to 450° F.

Do not freeze tofu or coat with arrowroot. Cut the tofu into bite-size pieces.

Line a baking sheet with nonstick foil. Place the tofu on the baking sheet. Spray the top of the tofu with canola oil.

Bake until tofu becomes golden brown around the edges, 20 to 25 minutes. Toss the tofu in the sauce, being sure to coat it completely. Serve warm.

vegetable risotto

MAKES 4 SERVINGS

QUICK AND EASY
MEAL IDEA:
CIAO, BELLA! (PAGE 44)

When dining out, I always get excited to see risotto on the menu, only to realize that it contains cream, Parmesan cheese, or both. Cooking the arborio rice slowly is the key to producing this rich and creamy risotto without the addition of dairy products. This is also one of those rare times when fresh herbs are essential. When you enjoy leftovers of this risotto, add a little more fresh marjoram after reheating it.

3 cups water

1 cup fresh green beans, trimmed, and cut into 1-inch pieces

6 baby asparagus spears, cut into 1-inch pieces

1 small zucchini, diced

1 small yellow squash, diced

5 cups vegetable stock or 5 cups boiling water mixed with vegetable bouillon

1 tablespoon extra virgin olive oil

1½ cups arborio or risotto rice

½ cup sliced leeks

1 teaspoon pepper

1 medium tomato diced

3 tablespoons roughly chopped fresh basil

4 tablespoons roughly chopped fresh marjoram

Bring 3 cups of water to a boil and add the green beans and asparagus. Return to a boil, reduce heat, cover, and simmer for 5 minutes. Add the zucchini and summer squash, and simmer 2 more minutes. Drain and set aside.

If using bouillon (preferred method): Bring 5 cups water to boil and add correct amount of bouillon according to instructions on package (use only enough bouillon for 4 cups of stock).

Bring stock or bouillon to a boil.

Reduce heat to low and keep the stock barely simmering.

Warm the oil in a medium sauce pan over medium heat. Add the arborio rice and leeks. Cook and stir for 2 minutes.

Slowly stir in 1 cup of hot stock and the pepper. Bring to a boil.

Reduce the heat to medium low, cook, and stir until almost all the liquid has been absorbed. Continue to add stock ½ cup at a time, stirring constantly after each addition until the liquid has been absorbed. Continue until the rice is tender and creamy.

Transfer the rice into a large pot over medium-low heat.

Add the cooked vegetables, tomatoes, basil, and 3 table-spoons marjoram. Cook and stir for 3 minutes or until thoroughly heated.

Transfer to serving bowls and garnish with the remaining marjoram.

wait-for-you stew

QUICK AND EASY
MEAL IDEA:
ONE-POT WONDER
(PAGE 45)

This is a veg'd-out twist on my mom's famous pot roast. Well, I guess it wasn't actually ever famous, but I always thought it was great, so that has to count for something. The best part about this recipe is that you can throw all the ingredients in the slow-cooker in the morning. When you get home from a long day at work you open your doors to the scent of a home-cooked meal, hot, ready and waiting for you. What could possibly be better than that?!

SEITAN:

¾ cup plus 2 tablespoons vital wheat gluten

¼ cup chickpea or soy flour

1 tablespoon nutritional yeast

1 teaspoon browning liquid, optional

1 cup water

SOUP BASE:

1 large russet or Yukon Gold potato, washed and cubed (skin on)

3 medium carrots, cut into large wedges

2 celery stalks, chopped

1 tablespoon nutritional yeast

1 teaspoon dried sage

⅛ teaspoon pepper

1 large garlic clove, minced

1 tablespoon vegan Worcestershire sauce

6 cups water

3 cubes vegan beef-flavored bouillon or enough to make 6 cups of non-beef broth

To make the seitan:

Combine all the seitan ingredients, stirring in water last, until a dough forms. Knead for 5 minutes and cut into small cubes (about ¼-inch square).

To make kneading easier, place the dough in a standing mixer with a dough hook and allow the mixer to do all the work for you.

To make the stew:

Add all the ingredients to a slow-cooker. Cook for 8 hours on low.

garden wrap

MAKES 4 WRAPS

QUICK AND EASY
MEAL IDEA:
WRAP IT UP (PAGE 42)

Wraps are a great variation on the traditional sandwich. You can pack a whole lot more in a large tortilla than you can between two slices of bread. I like this low-calorie wrap because it's everything I love about a fresh garden salad wrapped up in a light tortilla with the perfect spread.

SPREAD:

½ cup vegan mayonnaise

2 tablespoons nutritional yeast

1 teaspoon Dijon mustard

2 tablespoons chopped flat parsley

2 garlic cloves, minced

WRAP:

Four 8- to 12-inch flour tortillas

4 green leaf lettuce leaves

1 large tomato, sliced thin

4 large pepperoncini, drained, seeded, and sliced

½ cup sunflower sprouts

½ small onion, sliced thin

To make the spread:

Combine all the spread ingredients in a small bowl. Mix well and set aside.

To make the wrap:

Drop 3 tablespoons of spread on each tortilla and cover them, leaving ½-inch edges. Layer on the lettuce, tomato, pepperoncini, sprouts, and onion. Roll up the tortillas like you would a burrito. Serve immediately or chill for later eating.

sauces, dips, and dressings

Six-layer dip

MAKES 6 TO 8 SERVINGS

QUICK AND EASY
MEAL IDEA:
SAY QUESO! (PAGE 48)

This dip is quick, easy, and always a crowd favorite. If you serve it at a party, picnic, or backyard BBQ, a small group of people will quickly begin to gather around it, and before you know it, you have a dish filled with nothing but a piece of lettuce. I recommend layering this dish in a glass bowl or glass casserole dish to showcase the different layers.

1 cup vegan sour cream

¼ cup Taco Seasoning Mix (page 201)

2 cups vegetarian refried beans

2 medium avocados, diced and mashed

2 cups Chunky Fresh Salsa Picada (page 194)

1 cup shredded romaine, green leaf, or red leaf lettuce

½ cup green onions, chopped

Mix together the Taco Seasoning and sour cream.

Layer all ingredients in the following order (bottom to top):
    Refried beans
    Sour cream mixture
    Avocado
    Salsa
    Lettuce
    Green onions

plain ol' hummus

Hummus has become the unofficial mascot of the health food movement. My friends often tease me because they swear that all I eat is hummus. Besides just using hummus as a dip, I like to use it as a spread on sandwiches or whole-grain crackers instead of cheese, or as a substitute for vegan mayo in wraps.

One 14-ounce can garbanzo beans
¼ cup tahini
2 tablespoons flax oil
¼ cup lemon juice
2 garlic cloves, chopped
1¼ teaspoon ground cumin
¼ teaspoon sea salt
⅛ teaspoon pepper

Combine all ingredients in a food processor and process until smooth.

MAKES 2 CUPS

QUICK AND EASY
MEAL IDEA:
DILL OR NO DILL
(PAGE 42)

vegan ranch dressing

MAKES 2 CUPS

QUICK AND EASY
MEAL IDEA:
SOUP AND SALAD FULLY
LOADED (PAGE 43),
MOBILE PIZZERIA
(PAGE 43), TOO HOT TO
HANDLE (PAGE 43),
AND GIVE ME THAT FISH
(PAGE 46)

Although this is a salad dressing, I use it more often as a dip for fresh vegetables. If you would like it thinner, add 2 tablespoons to ¼ cup of water until you have your desired consistency.

½ cup raw cashews

1 cup raw macadamia nuts

3 tablespoons fresh lemon juice

2 or 3 garlic cloves, chopped

⅓ cup chopped celery

1 teaspoon fresh dill or ¼ teaspoon dried dill

1 teaspoon sea salt, or to taste

1½ teaspoons onion powder

¾ cup water

Put all the ingredients in a high-powered blender and blend until smooth. Store in an airtight container in the refrigerator for up to a week.

blue cheeze dressing

About a year before going vegan I began to fancy myself a cheese snob. I dabbled in Gouda, Edam, Blue cheese, Gruyère, Emmental—you name it, I loved it. The thought of eating one of these now makes my stomach turn, but I have developed a fondness for vegan cheese. Sheese brand makes a great blue cheese-style vegan cheese that goes great crumbled on salads or incorporated into a Blue Cheeze Dressing to go with Spicy Buffalo Bites (page 143) or as a salad dressing.

QUICK AND EASY
MEAL IDEA:
TUNO ME IS TO LOVE ME
(PAGE 42) AND GAME DAY
(PAGE 46)

½ cup vegan mayonnaise

½ cup vegan sour cream

1 tablespoon unsweetened plain soy milk

¼ teaspoon white pepper

¼ teaspoon onion powder

1½ teaspoons fresh lemon juice

½ teaspoon vegan Worcestershire sauce

⅛ teaspoon salt

Pinch of cayenne pepper

⅛ teaspoon garlic powder

¾ teaspoon sugar

3 ounces crumbled vegan blue cheese

Stir together all ingredients, adding crumbled cheese last. Refrigerate for at least 8 hours to allow the flavors to meld. Store in an airtight container for up to a week.

thousand island dressing

MAKES 1⅓ CUPS

QUICK AND EASY
MEAL IDEA:
IS IT CHILI IN HERE?
(PAGE 42), TUNI-ROLE
SUPPER (PAGE 47),
AND A THOUSAND MILES
FROM HOME (PAGE 47)

When I was growing up, my favorite salad dressing was Thousand Island. I loved it on a big green salad with sunflower seeds, tomatoes, and raisins. For over two years, my local grocery store carried a vegan thousand island dressing that tasted just like the one I grew up with, but one day they just abruptly stopped carrying it. I figured it couldn't be that hard to make my own vegan version, and as it turns out, I was right!

1 cup vegan mayonnaise

¼ cup ketchup

1 tablespoon white vinegar

1 tablespoon raw agave nectar

1 tablespoon plus 1 teaspoon sweet relish

½ teaspoon onion powder

⅛ teaspoon salt

Pinch of freshly ground black pepper

Whisk all the ingredients together in a small bowl. Cover and refrigerate for at least an hour but preferably overnight. Store in an airtight container for up to a week.

Simple balsamic vinaigrette

The key to good balsamic vinaigrette is the quality of the vinegar. I highly recommend splurging on a well-aged balsamic to add a robust flavor to your dressing. You can also use any remaining balsamic vinegar to marinate berries for Vanilla Bean Ice Cream with Balsamic Berries (page 217).

¼ cup extra virgin olive oil or flax oil

3 tablespoons balsamic vinegar

2 teaspoons minced shallot

1 garlic clove, minced

1 teaspoon fresh oregano, chopped

¼ teaspoon sea salt

⅛ teaspoon pepper

Whisk together all the ingredients. Store in an airtight container for up to a week.

MAKES ½ CUP

QUICK AND EASY
MEAL IDEA:
ITALIANO CLASSICO
(PAGE 46)

dill sauce

QUICK AND EASY
MEAL IDEA:

A FISHY SITUATION
(PAGE 42) AND DILL OR
NO DILL (PAGE 42)

Because dill is the highlight of this sauce I prefer to use fresh dill, but if you don't have immediate access to it, you can substitute 1 tablespoon dried dill. This sauce will keep for about four days in the refrigerator.

¼ cup vegan mayonnaise
¼ cup vegan sour cream
¼ cup chopped fresh dill

Stir together the mayonnaise and sour cream. Add the dill and stir together until thoroughly combined.

garlic herb spread

There's a vegan store here in Atlanta called Cosmo's Vegan Shoppe. It is every vegan's dream—vegan chocolate, marshmallows, a freezer packed with faux meats, dairy-free ice cream, and, of course, a refrigerator stocked with every type of vegan cheese you could imagine. The day Cosmo's started carrying Cheezly's Garlic Herb Cheese was one of the happiest days of my life. I skipped into the store, bought a pack, took it home, and just fifteen minutes later this Garlic Herb Spread was born. Just in case you don't have Cheezly's Garlic Herb Cheese readily available, you can shop at Cosmo's online at www.cosmosveganshoppe.com.

1 cup shredded Cheezly's Garlic Herb Cheese

⅓ cup vegan cream cheese

⅔ cup vegan sour cream

Stir all ingredients together in a small bowl.

MAKES 2 CUPS

QUICK AND EASY
MEAL IDEA:
THE ABCs OF LUNCH
(PAGE 41)

pizza sauce

MAKES 2 CUPS

QUICK AND EASY
MEAL IDEA:
MOBILE PIZZERIA
(PAGE 43)

Forty-five minutes might seem like a long time to simmer a pizza sauce, but as you taste it throughout the cooking process you'll see how the flavor develops over time. This sauce usually makes enough for two large pizzas, so I like to freeze 1 cup of it to use later.

One 14.5-ounce can diced tomatoes
One 6-ounce can tomato paste
½ teaspoon onion powder
½ teaspoon garlic powder
½ teaspoon dried thyme
½ teaspoon dried rosemary
1 teaspoon dried oregano
½ teaspoon sea salt
1 teaspoon sugar
¼ teaspoon pepper
1 bay leaf
1 teaspoon whole fennel seed

Put diced tomatoes and tomato paste in a blender and blend until smooth. Transfer to a medium saucepan over medium heat.

Stir in the remaining ingredients and bring to a simmer. Reduce the heat to low and simmer for 45 minutes to an hour, stirring occasionally. Remove the bay leaf and use the sauce as desired.

bbq sauce

After living in South Carolina for over two years I came to learn that BBQ is more than just a sauce, it's a way of life! I picked up BBQ sauce techniques such as the mustard-based sauce, the mayonnaise-based sauce, and your traditional ketchup-based sauce. Although I haven't perfected the art of the mustard- or mayonnaise-based sauces yet, I have learned how to make one heck of a ketchup-based BBQ sauce. Vegan Worcestershire sauce and traditional molasses are the secret ingredients that make this sauce really sing.

QUICK AND EASY
MEAL IDEAS:
SLOPPY JALOPY
(PAGE 43),
THE MEAN BEAN
(PAGE 42), AND
BACKYARD BBQ
(PAGE 45)

¼ cup diced white onion

1 tablespoon olive oil

1 garlic clove

2 cups ketchup

½ cup molasses

1½ teaspoons apple cider vinegar

¼ cup vegan Worcestershire sauce

1 tablespoons hickory liquid smoke

⅛ teaspoon cayenne pepper

Sauté the onion in olive oil over medium heat until it is soft, about 3 minutes. Add the garlic and sauté for an additional minute.

Add the remaining ingredients to a blender along with the garlic and onion, and puree until smooth.

cashew nut cheeze dip

MAKES 1½ CUPS

QUICK AND EASY
MEAL IDEA:
WRAP IT UP
(PAGE 42)

It is amazing how well cashews mimic the taste and texture of dairy products such as cream, milk, and cheese. This crowd-pleasing dip is great with chips at parties or as a healthy dip for raw vegetables in a midday snack. You can spread it on crackers or add it to sandwiches—the possibilities are endless.

1½ cups raw cashews
2 garlic cloves
¼ teaspoon turmeric
2 tablespoon lemon juice
4 whole oil-packed sun-dried tomatoes
⅛ teaspoon chili powder
¾ cup water
Dash of ground cumin

Blend all ingredients in a food processor or high-powered blender until smooth. This will keep for four days in the refrigerator.

enchilada sauce

Christmas 2007—the day I found out that my favorite enchilada sauce had chicken stock in it. Can you believe it?! Chicken stock! Agh! Once again, out of sheer desperation, I was forced to make a recipe of my own. The good part is that you get to enjoy it, too, chicken free.

3 cups vegetable stock

1½ tablespoon chili powder

½ teaspoon ground cumin

½ teaspoon garlic powder

½ teaspoon dried oregano

¼ teaspoon pepper

1 cup tomato sauce

¼ cup unbleached all-purpose flour

Put 2½ cups stock, chili powder, cumin, garlic powder, oregano, pepper, and tomato sauce in a medium saucepan and bring to a low boil. Reduce heat, cover, and simmer for 10 minutes, stirring frequently.

Whisk the flour into the remaining ½ cup of vegetable stock and add mixture to the enchilada sauce. Simmer for 5 minutes or until desired consistency is reached.

Use immediately or store in an airtight container in the refrigerator for up to 5 days.

MAKES 3 CUPS

QUICK AND EASY
MEAL IDEA:
ENCHILADA FIESTA
(PAGE 46) AND
BLACK BEAN BONANZA
(PAGE 45)

chunky fresh salsa picada

MAKES 4 CUPS

QUICK AND EASY
MEAL IDEA:
SAY QUESO! (PAGE 48)

Salsa Picada is a chunky version of traditional Mexican salsa. The big pieces of diced tomatoes stand out whether you're eating it alone or adding it to a multilayer dip like the Six-Layer Dip (page 182).

One 28-ounce can low-sodium diced tomatoes in juice

1 medium jalapeño, diced (use seeds for more heat)

½ cup diced red onion

½ medium green bell pepper, diced

½ cup loosely packed cilantro, chopped

Juice of ½ lime

Freshly ground black pepper, to taste

Dash of red pepper flakes, optional

Mix all the ingredients thoroughly. Cover the bowl with plastic wrap and refrigerate for at least 3 hours, or overnight for best results.

guacamole

I like my Guacamole rich and creamy with a couple of larger pieces of avocado to give it more texture. To achieve this, all you have to do is mash 1½ avocados and then stir in the remaining ½ diced avocado.

2 ripe avocados, diced

2 sun-dried tomatoes, softened in water, diced

¼ cup diced medium red onion

Juice of ½ lime

1 tablespoon cilantro, chopped

Dash of sea salt

Depending on the consistency you like, mash the avocados or just drop the diced avocados right in the bowl.

Add the remaining ingredients and stir. Cover and chill in the refrigerator for 30 minutes before eating.

MAKES 1½ CUPS

QUICK AND EASY
MEAL IDEAS:
FAT CHANCE (PAGE 42)
AND TORTILLA SQUARED
(PAGE 43)

mango salsa

QUICK AND EASY
MEAL IDEA:
TOFU OF THE SEA
(PAGE 44)

I'm horrible at cutting mangoes. No matter how many times I try to get it right, I still fail miserably. If you're as hopeless as me, feel free to use defrosted frozen mangoes in this recipe instead of fresh. But if you have the skills to cut and dice a fresh mango please feel free to use them, and know that I am very jealous of your mango-cutting skills.

1½ cups diced mangoes
½ medium jalapeño, diced (use seeds for more heat)
½ cup diced red onion
¼ cup loosely packed cilantro, chopped
Juice of ½ lime

Mix all ingredients thoroughly.

Cover the bowl with plastic wrap and refrigerate for at least 3 hours, or overnight for best results.

mushroom gravy

The funny thing about this recipe is that I've never really liked mushrooms or gravy, but somehow one day I found myself with a huge craving for brown rice with gravy. The vegan powder packets of faux chicken and beef gravy just weren't hitting the spot—thus, mushroom gravy was born!

5 cremini mushrooms, minced

5 shiitake mushrooms, minced

3 tablespoons canola oil

¼ cup unbleached all-purpose flour

2 tablespoons nutritional yeast

½ teaspoon black pepper

¼ teaspoon sea salt

1½ cups vegetable stock

Sauté the mushrooms in canola oil in a medium saucepan over medium heat for 2 minutes.

Stir in all the flour, nutritional yeast, pepper, and salt, and cook for an additional minute, stirring constantly.

Whisk in the stock ¼ cup at a time, until it reaches your desired thickness. If you want a smoother gravy, blend the gravy in a food processor or blender.

MAKES 2 CUPS

QUICK AND EASY
MEAL IDEA:
MAMA'S HOME COOKING
(PAGE 44)

nacho cheeze sauce

MAKES 1 CUP

QUICK AND EASY
MEAL IDEAS:
NACHO ORDINARY
DINNER (PAGE 48)
AND SOUTH BY
SOUTHWEST (PAGE 47)

Just because the name says nachos doesn't mean you have to stop there. This goes great over vegetables, or on a baked potato, veggie burgers, burritos, or anywhere else you're looking for a cheesy, slightly spicy kick.

1½ cups plain oat milk, soy milk, or water

½ cup nutritional yeast

¼ cup unbleached all-purpose flour

¼ cup canola oil or extra virgin olive oil

3 tablespoons tahini

1 teaspoon sea salt

¼ teaspoon garlic powder

½ teaspoon paprika

¼ teaspoon onion powder

½ teaspoon chili powder, or to taste

¼ teaspoon cayenne pepper

Whisk all the ingredients in a medium saucepan until the cheese is lump free. Cook until you have reached your desired consistency, stirring frequently.

pico de gallo

Pico de Gallo is very similar to Chunky Fresh Salsa Picada but with a fresh, more subdued flavor. It works perfectly as a dip or as a topping for tacos, burritos, and taco salads. Play around with this dish and try it on anything that could use an extra layer of flavor.

½ cup diced red onion

1 large tomato, diced

½ cup diced red bell pepper

Juice of ½ lime

¼ cup loosely packed cilantro, chopped or torn by hand

1 garlic clove, minced

1 teaspoon ground cumin

1 small jalapeño or 1 tablespoon canned green chilies (optional)

Put all the ingredients into a food processor and pulse until thoroughly combined, usually 4 to 5 pulses.

MAKES 2 CUPS

QUICK AND EASY
MEAL IDEA:
THE MIGHTY MUSHROOM
(PAGE 43)

sage gravy

MAKES 2 CUPS

This gravy is incredibly versatile. It goes well over Oven-fried Chik'n Seitan (page 140), cooked grains like quinoa and brown rice, as well as on Smashed Potatoes (page 88).

1 cup water

¼ cup unbleached all-purpose flour

1 cup vegetable stock

¼ cup nutritional yeast

1 tablespoon plus 1 teaspoon Bragg Liquid Aminos

½ teaspoon onion powder

1 tablespoon dried sage

½ teaspoon dried thyme

Whisk water and the flour in a medium saucepan over medium heat until the majority of the lumps have been whisked out.

Whisk in the remaining ingredients and bring to a low boil, reduce heat, and simmer until desired thickness is achieved.

taco seasoning mix

I swore by one particular brand of store-bought taco seasoning mix until one day I turned it over, looked at the ingredients, and realized that it was laden with MSG. Needless to say, my heart was broken. In the middle of a major taco craving, I took whatever I thought might go into a taco seasoning mix and threw it together. Thank God it turned out right the first time or I would've eaten just the taco shell that night.

3 tablespoons chili powder

1 teaspoon garlic powder

1 teaspoon onion powder

¼ teaspoon cayenne pepper or red pepper flakes

2 teaspoons paprika

2 tablespoons ground cumin

1 teaspoon sea salt

½ teaspoon pepper

Mix together all the ingredients in a small bowl. Store in an airtight container.

MAKES ⅓ CUP

QUICK AND EASY
MEAL IDEA:
BAJA CALIFORNIA DINNER
(PAGE 44)

tartar sauce

MAKES ⅓ CUP

QUICK AND EASY
MEAL IDEA:
TOFU OF THE SEA
(PAGE 44)

Buying tartar sauce was simply unheard of to my mother. There was never a time when we didn't have mayonnaise, relish, and mustard in the house and, therefore, never a reason to go out and buy a bottle of sauce that was composed of just these three simple ingredients.

¼ cup vegan mayonnaise

2 heaping tablespoons sweet relish, excess liquid drained off

½ teaspoon yellow mustard

Thoroughly combine all the ingredients in a small bowl. Refrigerate for 10 minutes and use on your favorite sandwiches.

teriyaki Sauce

As long as you have Teriyaki Sauce around you will always have the makings of a meal. Just cook up a little brown rice, steamed vegetables, and tofu, and you have yourself a complete dinner.

1 tablespoon arrowroot

¼ cup water

½ cup soy sauce

½ cup mirin

1 teaspoon minced fresh ginger (or ½ teaspoon ground ginger)

¼ teaspoon garlic powder

¼ cup agave nectar

Whisk the arrowroot and water and set aside.

Stir together the remaining ingredients in a medium saucepan over medium heat. Bring the mixture to a boil. Slowly stir in arrowroot slurry combination and heat, stirring constantly, until the mixture thickens and just starts to bubble.

MAKES 1 CUP

QUICK AND EASY
MEAL IDEA:
JAPANESE TAKEOUT
(PAGE 42)

thai peanut sauce

MAKES 2 CUPS

QUICK AND EASY
MEAL IDEA:
SOBA SIESTA (PAGE 42)

I don't really know if this is authentic Thai, but to me the finished product tastes "Thai-ish." Here it is . . . Thai-ish peanut sauce.

If using as a dip, I prefer tamarind paste; if using as a sauce, I prefer sriracha.

¾ cup creamy peanut butter

1 cup coconut milk

Juice of 1 lime, about 2 tablespoons

¼ cup vegetable stock

2 tablespoons water

1½ teaspoons rice vinegar

2 tablespoons Bragg Liquid Aminos or low-sodium soy sauce

1 teaspoon minced fresh ginger

1 garlic clove, minced

2 tablespoons brown sugar

½ teaspoon sriracha or ½ teaspoon tamarind paste

Mix all the ingredients in a medium bowl. This can be used as a dip or a sauce.

desserts

alicia's famous sweet potato pie

MAKES 8 SERVINGS

Yep, it's famous. I am the official sweet potato pie maker for my family. It isn't a holiday if my pie isn't there. This was a hard recipe to veganize, since traditionally, I used condensed milk and eggs whites to make my pies. But after a little tweaking, my famous sweet potato pie is now vegan and still a hit.

PIE CRUST:

1¼ cups unbleached all-purpose flour, plus more for dusting the work surface

¼ teaspoon sea salt

⅓ cup butter-flavored shortening or regular shortening

4 tablespoons cold water

PIE FILLING:

2 cups pureed sweet potatoes

½ cup granulated sugar

½ cup brown sugar

½ cup firm silken tofu

1¼ cups plain soy milk

1¼ teaspoons ground cinnamon

½ teaspoon freshly grated nutmeg

2 tablespoons unbleached all-purpose flour

Preheat the oven to 375° F.

To make the pie crust:

Pulse the flour and salt in a food processor just to disburse the salt. Add the shortening and run the food processor until shortening is completely incorporated and mixture resembles a grainy flour or cornmeal. Slowly add cold water, 1 tablespoon at a time, just until a dough has formed. You may not need the entire 4 tablespoons of water. Scrape down the sides of the bowl with a spatula and give two more quick pulses. On a lightly floured surface roll dough out to about ⅛-inch thick and approximately 12 inches in diameter. Carefully transfer the dough to a 9-inch pie pan and press into the pan.

To make the pie filling:

Put all the ingredients in a blender and blend on the highest speed until smooth, about 2 minutes.

Pour the filling into the pie crust. Cover the exposed pie crust with aluminum foil to prevent it from browning too quickly.

Bake for 55 to 60 minutes, until a toothpick comes out it clean. Remove it from the oven, and allow the pie to cool for at least an hour (the filling is VERY hot). Refrigerate for at least another an hour, and serve chilled.

COOK'S TIP:

Roast sweet potatoes for 50 minutes, scoop out the flesh, and put it directly into the blender. It's one hundred times better than the canned stuff.

all-purpose cupcakes

These cupcakes are chameleons. They go with just about any frosting you can come up with, plus sprinkles, the whole nine yards. When you just need cupcakes without all the frills, these are the ones for you.

½ cup shortening, plus more for the cupcake tins

¾ cup soy milk

1 teaspoon vanilla extract

1 cup sugar

¼ cup unsweetened applesauce

1 cup unbleached all-purpose flour

¾ cup whole wheat pastry flour

2½ teaspoons baking powder

½ teaspoon sea salt

Preheat the oven to 375° F. Grease a twelve-muffin tin with shortening or line with paper liners.

Cream the shortening with the milk, vanilla, sugar, and applesauce.

Combine the all-purpose flour, whole wheat pastry flour, baking powder, and salt in a large bowl.

Add the flour mixture ½ cup at a time to the creamed shortening mix, mixing well after each addition.

Fill cupcake cups three-quarters full and bake for 15 to 18 minutes, until a toothpick comes out clean. Cool fully before frosting.

I can rationalize anything. For example, oatmeal cookies have oats, nondairy milk, applesauce, raisins, and walnuts. That sounds like a complete, nutritious breakfast to me! Surely these cookies have less sugar than most commercial children's cereal. So if there happen to be a dozen or so oatmeal cookies sitting on the counter and I grab a couple before I run out the door in the morning, I cut myself some slack and just pretend it's a real breakfast.

MAKES 2 DOZEN COOKIES

¾ cup butter-flavored shortening

½ cup granulated sugar

¾ cup brown sugar

¼ cup unsweetened applesauce

¼ cup plain soy milk or oat milk

1 teaspoon vanilla extract

1½ cups quick oats

1 ½ cup unbleached all-purpose flour

½ teaspoon baking powder

1 teaspoon baking soda

1 teaspoon sea salt

¾ cup raisins

¾ cup chopped walnuts or pecans

Preheat the oven to 350° F.

Cream the shortening, granulated sugar, brown sugar, and applesauce with an electric mixer.

Stir in soy milk and vanilla. Then add the quick oats and stir until incorporated.

Combine the flour, baking powder, baking soda, and salt in a separate bowl. Add this mixture to the shortening, ½ cup at a time, until completely combined. Fold in the raisins and walnuts.

Form about a tablespoon of dough into 1½-inch balls, and place them about 2 inches apart on a cookie sheet.

Bake for 12 minutes for a chewy cookie and up to 14 for a crispier cookie.

peach cobbler

Peach Cobbler has to be one of the quickest desserts to assemble. I use frozen peaches instead of fresh ones to cut down on the time and turn my attention to my favorite part of every cobbler and pie—the crust! Enjoy this cobbler à la mode with Vanilla Bean Ice Cream (page 217).

Just a warning: when I tried out this cobbler on my parents for Christmas, it resulted in the three of us lying on our respective couches, rubbing our bellies, with silly grins on our faces in what I like to call a "cobbler coma."

COBBLER CRUST:

2½ cups unbleached all-purpose flour

¾ teaspoon sea salt

⅔ cup plus 1 tablespoon butter-flavored shortening, or a combination of nonhydrogenated margarine and shortening

7 tablespoons cold water

PEACH FILLING:

Three 10-ounce packages frozen peaches, thawed

½ cup granulated sugar

½ cup brown sugar

¼ teaspoon ground cinnamon

¼ teaspoon grated nutmeg

1½ teaspoons arrowroot or cornstarch

1 tablespoon nonhydrogenated margarine

Preheat the oven to 350° F.

To make the cobbler crust:

Put the flour and salt into a food processor with a metal blade and give two quick pulses to disburse the salt. Add the shortening and run the food processor until the shortening is completely incorporated and the mixture resembles a grainy flour or cornmeal. Add cold water 1 tablespoon at a time just until a dough has formed, pulsing between each addition. Separate the dough into two balls, one slightly larger than the other. On a lightly floured surface roll out each dough ball from the center to the edge. Use the larger dough ball to make the bottom crust and the smaller ball for the top crust.

If you have a little extra time on your hands or don't have a food processor, you can cut the shortening into the flour mixture with a pastry blender, then add water 1 tablespoon at a time just until dough forms. Then proceed as above.

To make the cobbler:

Lightly grease an 8×8-inch baking dish and lay down the bottom crust, making sure to cover the bottom and sides of the dish completely.

In a medium bowl, mix the peaches, sugar, brown sugar, cinnamon, and nutmeg until the peaches are well coated. Sprinkle the arrowroot over the peaches and stir until dissolved.

Pour the peach mixture into the prepared baking dish. Place small bits of margarine on top of the peaches and cover with the second pie crust, making sure to close all edges.

Bake for 45 minutes to 1 hour or until the crust is golden brown.

peach fritters

This recipe works great with peaches, pears, or apples. You can also use frozen and thawed peaches to cut down on the prep time.

Canola oil for frying

2-egg equivalent powdered egg replacer, prepared according to package directions, and whisked until foaming

½ cup plain soy milk or almond milk

¼ cup brown sugar

½ cup unbleached all-purpose flour

¼ teaspoon baking soda

1½ cups (or one 10-ounce package frozen) peeled, sliced peaches

Cinnamon

Confectioners' sugar

In a large pot or deep-fryer, heat the oil to 375° F.

Stir the soy milk, brown sugar, flour, and baking soda into the prepared egg replacer. Add the peaches to the batter and coat well.

Fry battered peaches in oil for 2 to 3 minutes, turning once, until lightly browned. Drain the peaches on paper towels.

Dust with cinnamon and confectioners' sugar and serve.

peanut butter cookies

If your local grocery store or health food store has freshly ground peanut butter available, use it for this recipe. The fresher the peanut butter, the better the cookie.

MAKES 2 DOZEN COOKIES

½ cup granulated sugar

½ cup brown sugar

½ cup creamy peanut butter

½ cup butter-flavored shortening

¼ cup unsweetened applesauce

2 tablespoons plain soy milk

1½ cups unbleached all-purpose flour, sifted

¾ teaspoon baking soda

½ teaspoon sea salt

Preheat the oven to 375° F.

Blend the granulated sugar, brown sugar, peanut butter, shortening, and soy milk with an electric mixer until creamy. Then beat in the applesauce until it is well incorporated.

Mix the flour, baking soda, and salt in a separate bowl. Add this mixture to the peanut butter mixture, ½ cup at a time, beating well after each addition.

Use a teaspoon to scoop out pieces of dough and roll them into 1-inch balls. Place the balls about 2 inches apart on an ungreased cookie sheet, and flatten them in a crisscross pattern with a fork tip.

Bake 10 minutes or until a light golden brown. Remove from baking sheet, cool, and enjoy.

Sugar Cookies

MAKES 18 COOKIES

If I had blue hair it would be almost impossible to tell the difference between me and Cookie Monster. There are very few recipes that I have memorized, and this is one of them. These cookies don't need any frosting or sprinkled sugar topping, just a cold glass of soy or oat milk.

¼ cup unsweetened applesauce

1 cup sugar

½ cup butter-flavored shortening

1½ teaspoons plain oat milk or soy milk

1 teaspoon vanilla extract

1½ cups unbleached all-purpose flour

1½ teaspoons baking powder

½ teaspoon sea salt

Preheat the oven to 350° F.

Beat the applesauce sugar, shortening, and soy milk with an electric mixer on high. Blend until light and fluffy. Add the vanilla and blend for an additional 30 seconds.

In a separate bowl, stir together the flour, baking powder, and salt.

Sift the flour mixture into the applesauce mixture, ½ cup at a time, and beat with an electric mixer on low speed after each addition until all the flour is incorporated.

There are three different ways to proceed with this dough: make drop cookies, make shaped cookies, or freeze it for later use. These three methods follow.

Drop Cookies (preferred method):

Scoop 1 tablespoon of dough into your hand, roll the dough into a ball, and place balls 2 inches apart on an ungreased cookie sheet. Flatten the balls until they are about ¼ inch thick and bake for 10 minutes for chewier cookies or 12 minutes for crisp.

Shaped Cookies:

Lightly flour a cutting board (or other large, smooth, non-porous surface), and roll the dough out ¼ inch thick. Do not knead dough. Cut out desired shapes, place on an ungreased cookie sheet, and bake for 10 minutes for chewier cookies or 12 minutes for crisp.

Frozen Cookies:

Divide the dough in two. Shape each piece into a log about 2 inches across, roll each log in wax or parchment paper, and freeze. When you are ready to bake cookies, slice dough into ¼-inch-thick pieces, and follow the directions for making drop cookies, above.

COOK'S TIP:

These cookies are soft and chewy, but if you prefer a crisper cookie, use only 1 or 2 tablespoons of applesauce.

pear crisps for two

These Pear Crisps are the perfect autumn dessert. Fresh Bartlett or Bosc pears take this dish to a level that apples simply cannot touch. However, if all you have on hand are apples, you can use them instead.

Canola oil for the ramekins

¼ cup vegan cream cheese

¼ cup brown sugar

¼ teaspoon grated nutmeg

2 large Bartlett or Bosc pears, peeled, cored and roughly chopped

¼ cup oatmeal

¼ cup unbleached all-purpose flour

Handful of raw pecans, roughly chopped

¼ cup nonhydrogenated margarine

Preheat the oven to 375° F.

Wipe down two 9- or 10-ounce ramekins with canola oil.

Combine the cream cheese, 2 tablespoons brown sugar, and nutmeg. Stir in the pears and spoon into the ramekins.

Mix the oatmeal, flour, 2 tablespoons brown sugar, and pecans. Add the margarine and cut it in with a pastry blender or fork. Sprinkle this mixture over the pears.

Place the ramekins on a baking sheet covered with foil to catch any drippings. Bake for 45 minutes or until the pears are bubbling. Serve warm.

vanilla bean ice cream with balsamic berries

On hot California summer days, my mother would get out the big wooden ice cream maker, fill it with rock salt, cream, sugar, eggs, and vanilla, and churn it by hand for thirty minutes so we could enjoy fresh, homemade ice cream. Ice cream makers have come a long way since the '80s. Now all you have to do is blend your ingredients, pour them into the ice cream maker, and in twenty or thirty minutes you have homemade vegan ice cream.

MAKES 1 QUART

1½ cups plain soy milk

½ cup plus 2 tablespoons sugar

1½ cups plain, unsweetened soy yogurt

1 vanilla bean, split lengthwise

Whisk the soy milk with the sugar until the sugar is completely dissolved. Whisk soy yogurt into soy milk mixture.

Open the vanilla bean and scrape out the seeds with a spoon. Whisk the vanilla seeds into soy milk mixture, leaving no lumps.

Pour the whole thing into an electric ice cream maker and prepare according to manufacturer's directions. This usually takes 25 to 30 minutes to freeze.

Balsamic Berries:

MAKES 2 SERVINGS

⅓ cup blueberries

⅓ cup raspberries

⅓ cup blackberries

⅓ cup balsamic vinegar

Wash all the berries and marinate in balsamic vinegar for 30 minutes.

Drain the vinegar and serve over Vanilla Bean Ice Cream or whatever delicious treat you desire.

yellow cake with chocolate icing

MAKES 8 SERVINGS

I was never a big fan of sweets growing up, partly because I was an extremely hyperactive child and my poor parents did their best to keep sugar and caffeine away from me. Ironically, the very first recipe I created was for cookies, and my one weakness is Yellow Cake with Chocolate Icing. I am very proud to present to you my favorite cake of all time. I hope you enjoy it as much as I have.

2 cups unbleached all-purpose flour, sifted

2½ teaspoons baking powder

1 teaspoon sea salt

½ cup butter-flavored shortening

1½ cups sugar

½ cup unsweetened applesauce

1¼ cups plain oat milk or soymilk

1 teaspoon vanilla extract

Preheat the oven to 350° F.

Combine the flour, baking powder, and salt.

In a separate bowl, cream the shortening sugar, applesauce, ½ cup oat milk, and vanilla with an electric mixer until fluffy. Add the remaining oat milk and mix for 30 seconds.

Add the flour mixture to the shortening ½ cup at a time until all the flour is incorporated.

Here is a fork in the road. You can bake this batter in two 9-inch-round pans to make a layer cake, a 9×13-inch pan for a single-layer cake, or in cupcake tins. Choose your path, and follow the directions below.

Layer Cake:

Oil two 9-inch-round pans. Divide the batter evenly in the two pans and bake for 20 to 25 minutes, until a toothpick inserted into the center comes out clean. Cool for 5 minutes, and remove from the pans. Allow cakes to cool completely. Cover the top of the first layer with Chocolate Icing, then top with the second cake, and completely cover the entire cake with the remaining icing in a thin layer.

Single-layer Cake:

Oil a 9×13-inch pan and bake for 30 to 35 minutes, until a toothpick inserted into the center comes out clean. Cool completely, and spread Chocolate Icing evenly over the cake.

Cupcakes:

Lightly oil a cupcake pan or fill with cupcake liners. Fill each cup three-quarters full. Bake for 15 to 20 minutes, or until a toothpick inserted into the center comes out clean. Spread Chocolate Icing evenly over each cupcake.

CHOCOLATE ICING:

½ cup plus 1 tablespoon butter-flavored shortening

½ cup vegan cream cheese

1 teaspoon vanilla extract

⅓ cup unsweetened cocoa powder

3 cups confectioners' sugar

Whip the shortening and cream cheese with an electric mixer for 4 to 5 minutes, until light and fluffy. Add the vanilla and mix for an additional minute. Slowly add the cocoa powder until completely incorporated. Add the sugar 1 cup at a time until completely incorporated and the icing is smooth. Allow to sit at room temperature for 5 minutes before use.

Sweetgrass Snickerdoodles

MAKES 2 DOZEN COOKIES

These soft, chewy cookies are named after my favorite spa in Atlanta. I can't eat a whole batch myself, so while testing the recipe I brought some to the spa on one of my monthly visits. Everyone loved them and the cookies were gone in minutes. So thank you to everyone at Sweetgrass for being my first testers for Sweetgrass Snickerdoodles.

½ cup nonhydrogenated margarine

½ cup shortening

½ cup unsweetened applesauce

1 cup granulated sugar

½ cup light brown sugar

2¾ cups unbleached all-purpose flour

1½ teaspoons cream of tartar

1 teaspoon baking soda

1 teaspoon baking powder

¼ teaspoon sea salt

GARNISH:

¼ cup sugar

1 tablespoon ground cinnamon

Preheat the oven to 350° F.

Cream the margarine and shortening with the applesauce and sugars. In a separate bowl combine the flour, cream of tartar, baking soda, baking powder, and salt.

Combine the dry ingredients with the creamed mixture ½ cup at a time and mix with an electric mixer until all the dry ingredients are incorporated.

Chill the dough for about 10 minutes in the refrigerator.

Combine ¼ cup granulated sugar with the cinnamon.

Scoop 1-inch balls of dough with a teaspoon. Roll each ball in the cinnamon sugar mixture, coating all sides.

Place on a baking sheet about 1½ inches apart and bake for 12 minutes for chewy cookies and up to 15 minutes for a crisper cookie.

Remove from baking sheet, cool, and enjoy.

acknowledgments

THANK YOU TO the two most supportive people in my life, my parents, John and Linda. You guys have stuck firmly by my side for twenty-nine long years and I wouldn't be anywhere if it were not for your love and support. Dad, thank you for trying every dish that I made for you guys, and Mom, thank you for trying tofu again and again until you finally liked it.

Thank you to Pauline Neuwirth for being my tireless advocate and for smiling through all our technical difficulties. Never-ending thanks to Matthew Lore for taking a chance on my little project and helping me turn it into an amazing book. Thank you to an incredibly talented food photographer and stylist, Lori Maffei, for your amazing work in this book.

Thank you, Arden Zinn, for opening my eyes to veganism. You have truly changed my life.

Thank you to all the people who tasted, tested, and reviewed my food over the last three years. You have been the driving force that has kept the food in this book accessible, easy to make, and, of course, delicious. A special thanks to my fourth favorite omnivore (mom, dad, and grandmother—you are my top three), Andrew, for trying every dish I put before you, even the ones that still needed a lot of tweaking, and for providing me with the inspiration for Banana Pancakes.

index

C

Cabbage, on something's fishy tacos, 165
Caesar salad with sourdough croutons, 98–99
Cake, yellow, with chocolate icing, 218–19
Calcium and iron sources, 7
Calcium deficiency myth, 6–8
California-style biscuits, 60–63
Candied yams, 79
Cannellini bean soup, 115
Cantaloupe, in cucumber smoothie, 34
Caper and lemon linguine, 150
Carrots
   agave-glazed, 76
   -and raisin muffins, 59
   in spicy soba noodles in peanut sauce, 153
   in stew, 178–79
   in teriyaki rice bowl, 167
   in vegetable lasagna, 156–57
Cashew nut(s), 85
   -cheeze dip, 192
   in mac and cheeze, 84–85
   -milk, 72
   in ranch dressing, 184
Casserole dishes, 28
Cheese, vegan, 11–12, 185, 189
   on avocado melt panini, 120
   in baked potato soup, 104–5
   in baked ziti, 123
   blue cheeze dressing, 185
   on chicken patties or nuggets, 158–59
   for "Egg" MacGuffins, 64
   in enchiladas, 126–27, 128
   on filet o' tofish sandwiches, 134–35
   grilled cheese, 122
   in grits cakes, 148
   mac and cheeze, 84–85
   in mex burritos, 137
   nacho cheeze sauce, 198
   for nachos, 124, 125
   on "pepperoni" mini pizzas, 151
   spinach and cheeze scramble, 68–69
   in spinach lasagna, 154–55

on sun-dried tomato and roasted red pepper panini, 162
   in tuno casserole, 170–71
   on tuno melt, 169
   in vegetable lasagna, 156–57
   in veggie casserole, 172
"Chicken" patties and nuggets (store bought), 158–59
Chickpea flour, 21
   in stew, 178
Chickpeas. *See* Garbanzo beans
Chik'n from tofu, 174–75
Chik'n seitan, 138
   for chicken patties and nuggets, 158–59
   in enchiladas, 126–27
   fried, 139
   in orange chik'n, 174–75
   oven-fried, 140
   pecan-crusted cutlets, 142
   sloppy josephs, 144–45
   spicy buffalo bites, 143
   spicy oven-fried, 141
Chili, 129
Chocolate icing, yellow cake with, 218–19
Coconut milk
   in corn chowder, 102
   in spicy pumpkin soup, 111
   in Thai peanut sauce, 204
Coconut water, in tropical cress smoothie, 36
Collard greens, 80
Comfort food to go, 41–44
Cookies
   oatmeal, 209
   peanut butter, 213
   snickerdoodles, 220
   sugar, 214–15
Corn, 89
   coconut corn chowder, 102
   in enchiladas sin queso, 128
   in mex burritos, 137
   -salad, fresh, 103
   spicy, 89
   in tortilla soup, 114
   in winter bean soup, 115
Cornbread, 90
Cornbread mix, 90
Corn flakes, in pecan-crusted seitan cutlets, 142
Costa Rica, 66

Couscous, in veggie casserole, 172
Cow's milk, 15–16
Cranberries, in mango cranrugula smoothie, 39
Croissant sandwiches, 163
Cucumber smoothie, 34
Cupcakes, 208, 218–19

D

Dandelion greens, 37
Dandelion smoothie, 37
Dates, adding to smoothies, 32
Dessert recipes, 206–20
Detoxifying with green vegetables, 32, 39
Dilla, 132
Dill sauce, 121, 188
Dinner recipes, 120–80
Dinnertime suggestions, 44–48
Dip recipes, 182–83, 192
Dulse, in tuno casserole, 170

E

"Egg" MacGuffins, 64
Egg replacer, 19
   in peach fritters, 212
   in pecan-crusted seitan cutlets, 142
   silken tofu as, 11
   in sweet potato waffles, 52–53
Enchiladas, 126–27, 128
Enchilada sauce, 193
Energy-boosting green smoothies, 31–32
   recipes, 33–39
Expense of vegan food, 6

F

Farmers' markets, 6
Fettuccine Alfredo, 130–31
Filet o' tofish sandwiches, 134
Flax oil, 13
Flaxseeds, 13
   in breakfast power smoothie, 56
   in carrot and raisin muffins, 59
   in green goblin drink mix, 74
Flour(s), 21, 58
   buckwheat flour, 153

226   INDEX

11-12-12

about the author

ALICIA C. SIMPSON has been cooking since she was tall
enough to reach the stove. She is the creator of the popular blog
Vegan Guinea Pig and has been featured in the documentary *I'm
Vegan*. She is also the author of *Quick and Easy Vegan Celebrations*.
Alicia lives in Atlanta.

www.aliciacsimpson.com